THE DYSFUNCTIONAL WORKPLACE

The Dysfunctional Workplace

THEORY, STORIES, AND PRACTICE

———

Seth Allcorn
and
Howard F. Stein

UNIVERSITY OF MISSOURI PRESS
Columbia

Contents

PART THREE CONCLUSIONS

Foreword

In this first in a series of forthcoming books from the Center for the Study of Organizational Change (CSOC) and the University of Missouri Press, Seth Allcorn and Howard F. Stein want us (all) to acknowledge the nonrational side of human nature inside and outside professional and organizational life. They assume—and I tend to agree—that such an acknowledgment is critical to enhancing the emotional well-being, humaneness, and competence of the workforce. No doubt, this is a tall order. The successful leap from insight and awareness to positive change has always posed a challenge to those of us who have spent our careers as scholar-practitioners in the field of organization studies and change.

To acknowledge what Allcorn and Stein call the darker side of human nature requires embracing imperfections and defensiveness, the latter meant to cloak and rationalize our errors of judgment, flawed characters, and questionable actions. Leaders and executives, in particular, according to the authors, need to assume responsibility in a way that acknowledges their *actual* humanity, not some fantasied and idealized version. Mature and humane leadership and management demand a level of consciousness, emotional intelligence, and authenticity, if you will, from which reflective executives might manage and contain their own narcissism, which is fueled by the heady fumes of inordinate power and authority.

The stories shared by the authors in this book are meant to proffer a mirror of recognition and identification, however dark, disappointing, and demystifying that might be, for leaders and followers, executives, managers, and workers (present and future). These stories are meant for the perpetrators and the victims of psychological abuse and oppression in the twenty-first-century workplace.

Storytelling is the authors' method of choice, and they tell these stories through a contemporary psychoanalytic lens. Indeed, a relational theory of mind and meaning often relies on narrative structure. Their storytelling attempts to capture a moment in time and space that best represents the meaning and experience of organizational membership. The authors want us to assume, based on their observations and experiences, that storytelling clarifies an individual's place in the relational politics and culture of organizations as well as that person's opposition to it. Illuminating the boundary between self and organization may be critical for people traumatized by mistreatment, neglect, and abuse in the workplace. Inherent in storytelling is the relationship between storyteller and audience that produces shared meanings and consensual validation, what we would describe psychoanalytically as processes of identification and empathy. The psychosocial processes of storytelling promote a sense of well-being simply through human contact and construction of context for one's sense of self. Storytelling is not only textual, it is experiential, meaningful, and contextual. As the authors use it here, it captures the thematic relational patterns of key participants that shape the quality of work life as well as the participants' unconscious assumptions and the motives behind their decisions, actions, strategies, and policies.

Organizations are relational, experiential, and perceptual. Storytelling gets us closer to the heart and pulse of organizational identity and therefore closer to the meaning of members' perceptions and their shared psychological reality. As you read these stories, consider what they tell us about ourselves and the level of consciousness, humility, and morality necessary for responsible and "good enough" organizational leadership.

This book alerts us to the damage, and often irreparable individual hurt and societal costs, of toxic and narcissistic executives and managers. In an era of organizational change by fiat, change management, re-engineering, downsizing, technology transfer, management information systems, and appreciative inquiry—to use all the buzzwords—we desperately need a contrary approach that is honest, reality-based, critical, bilateral, and constructively confrontational. Storytelling as presented here is not a form of research or consultation performed and directed on

behalf of executives and executive power; rather, these stories are intended to genuinely expose and illuminate without censure the real-life consequences of unconscious and taken-for-granted power and authority.
Allcorn and Stein have accomplished that.

Michael A. Diamond, Ph.D.
SERIES EDITOR
ADVANCES IN ORGANIZATIONAL PSYCHODYNAMICS

Preface

This is a book of stories about the American workplace. The stories are about personal experiences and meanings of "what it is like to work here." The stories are not the usual hard data that are collected and published in most business, management, and organizational journals. In fact, the stories are mostly about what goes *unsaid* in official research, scholarship, and organizational mission statements and strategic plans. The stories are a kind of organizational underbelly, the dark side of organizational life. This book helps to fill a void in literature on organizations, one that has also been identified in recent years by Yiannis Gabriel in his essays and books on organizational stories and storytelling (1999, 2011, 2012).

The stories come from our experiences as consultants, as a university and health sciences center executive (Allcorn), and as professor and applied ethnographer (Stein), and as listeners to others' stories and observers of workplaces. The stories are about us and others, about our inner response to our work experience and that of others. It is about the intersubjective (unconscious-to-unconscious) dance between storyteller and story listener. The stories really did happen. We have disguised names and places to protect the confidentiality of the people in the stories and those who told us their stories. We dutifully note that the stories told are based on memory and therefore are unavoidably imperfect retellings of events; further, they contain as well unconscious elements that we as authors bring to storytelling (Spence, 1982). They are, then, representative of what happened.

We bring a psychodynamic perspective to our work and to understanding these stories. This psychoanalytic perspective is not an add-on to more conventional ways of studying and understanding organizations, but rather it is a way of broadening and deepening our access to the inner

xiii

experience of the workplace. Human nature and the unconscious per-meate every aspect of organizational life. Our hope is that the meanings, emotions, fantasies, and conflicts that we unearth in the stories will be as familiar to the reader as they became to us.

We would like to offer a story about how we came to write this book. We have been colleagues and friends since the mid-1990s, when we first participated in a longitudinal study of the large-scale downsizing of "General Hospital" and soon thereafter wrote a book with Michael Diamond and Howell Baum. The book was called *The Human Cost of a Management Failure: Downsizing at General Hospital* (1996). The two of us have collaborated on a number of research and writing projects since then, most recently on the unconscious meanings of the widespread economic practice of deregulation.

In mid-2013 we began regular weekly visits on Skype. Both of us had recently retired and were searching for meaningful ways to continue our work on organizational life. Our rich conversations over Skype triggered memories and stories in each of us—from our own workplace experienc-es, consultation, observation, organizational leadership, and from those who told us their stories. We were struck by how hard it would be to make these stories up, which became a recurring theme in our work. For months we e-mailed drafts of stories, and discussion of the stories, back and forth. The stories snowballed.

Part of the process involved each and both of us remembering, and to an extent working through, our own experiences in multiple roles in organizations for more than four decades. Our Skype visits often had the quality of free association, sharing fantasies, and processing the thoughts and emotions that surfaced. We trusted that we were going in the right direction. We trusted the process—and each other. We eagerly looked forward to our weekly meetings and corresponded by e-mail during the interval. Somewhere in this process we thought of assembling a book of stories.

We thought that a collection of workplace stories would be of value to other people—that the stories would be at once a source of informa-tion and a source for becoming more whole in life and work. We hope that our stories will rekindle the reader's own stories for reflection and to some degree inner healing, as well as an increased ability to listen to other people's often-disturbing stories of organizational life. Listening is important in that it creates the receptive medium into which the teller places the story.

Our stories about the dark side of organizational life and your stories of a similar nature together create a sense of mutual validation. The stories are accounts of what really happened, even if it is difficult to believe that they did, and even if it is difficult to persuade other employees and leaders that they did. It is in this sense of mutual validation that it is possible to step back for a few moments to reflect upon and process the personal harm, harm to others, and workplace suffering that we and you have experienced and observed.

Our work here, much like the book on downsizing at General Hospital (1996), is also a larger story about the American workplace, past, present, and future, and about human nature beneath it. The intimate stories shared here are a microcosm of the culture and era we all inhabit—and of being human. We invite readers to join us in what is truly a close inspection of work life often ignored by researchers and all too often dismissed as mere anomalies by management and human resource professionals.

This book is suitable for multiple audiences. In particular, students and scholars of organizational life and consultants to organizations will find it informative and that it raises important questions about organizational dynamics. Similarly, it will make a contribution to students and faculty of graduate schools of organizational studies, management, government and public affairs. By providing an example of how qualitative methodology can be used to understand organizational life, it will also be of interest to researchers. Additionally, it will make a valuable contribution to programs and courses in psychology that have as their focus understanding organizations and human behavior in the workplace. The scope of the book includes courses in applied psychoanalysis, psychohistory, anthropology (especially psychological anthropology and applied anthropology), sociology, political psychology, and American studies. Finally, the book extends to an even wider circle of readers who wish to make sense of their own organizational experiences.

This book also has significance beyond the North American market. Although the stories themselves are drawn from experiences in the United States, they implicitly address increasingly global experiences as well, especially in Europe and developing countries. Certainly, nations and ethnic groups have their own cultural styles of leadership, followership, and organizational culture. However, the ubiquitous process of globalization involves not only the spread and cultural diffusion of specific industries and products but also the adoption, if not imposition, of American corporate leadership styles and group interaction. Further, we stress pan-human issues and processes in human life that encompass organizational behavior anywhere.

August 2014

Seth Allcorn, Ph.D.
Columbia, MO

Howard F. Stein, Ph.D.
Oklahoma City, OK

Acknowledgments

We wish to acknowledge the ongoing support and encouragement of Dr. Michael A. Diamond, director of the Center for the Study of Organizational Change and professor of Organizational Analysis and Change, Harry S Truman School of Public Affairs, University of Missouri, Columbia, and of our mutual colleague Dr. Carrie M. Duncan, Teaching Assistant Professor, also at the Truman School of Public Affairs. They are two amazing human beings. We are grateful to David Rosenbaum, director of the University of Missouri Press, for his enthusiastic advocacy of this book and his helpful navigation of the review and publication process. Howard Stein also wishes to acknowledge the support provided by his wife, Rev. Dr. Nance Cunningham, during the writing and production of this book, and he gratefully acknowledges the comfort provided by his cat, Luke, during the countless hours Howard spent at the computer or writing in his chair with pen and paper. We also appreciate the feedback we received from Becky Farris and Stephanie Young, who located some of our stories in their lives, confirming for us the importance of sharing the stories. We also want to acknowledge the outstanding creative assistance provided by Bruce Duncan in developing the three figures. We truly appreciate a job well done.

Last, we wish to acknowledge those dysfunctional, and not infrequently toxic, leaders and organizations that provided us with the experiences and stories we have shared here. Human nature has both a light and inspiring side and a dark side. In a sense we cannot be truly thankful for the dark experiences and stories, but rather we are thankful we have an opportunity to share them in a thoughtful, reflective way and to learn from sharing them. Rather than deny the existence of the dark side of human nature, we must embrace it for what it is and, we hope, do so in a way that can be understood and make life at work less toxic.

PART ONE

THEORY

The first chapter in part 1 sets the context of the book by underscoring the role of storytelling throughout human history. Stories are in a sense statements about who we are. They provide rich and varied insights into ourselves, others, and the world around us, including the workplace. Chapter 2 provides an overview of different perspectives and approaches to understanding workplace stories. It examines the various ways stories in the workplace and elsewhere may be understood and used, in some instances for the explicit purpose of managing organizations. In Chapter 3 we introduce definitions and discuss a select number of concepts drawn from psychoanalytic theory that we will use to understand the stories. Further, our first story uses the definitions of the concepts in terms of how they may be used to understand life at work. The concepts can be readily understood and appreciated for their contribution to understanding one's self, others, and groups in the workplace.

CHAPTER I

Stories from the Workplace
An Introduction

Life in many ways is about stories. We tell stories to convey what life is about. The answers to the questions "What did you do today?" and "What was life like for you today?" are stories about daily adventures, happenings and events, and conversations with others. These stories might be said to be a discontinuous narrative. The books, newspapers, and magazines we read; the televised content we watch; and much of the Internet content we are exposed to all tell us stories. What we hear about others are stories. Stories are those widely used forms of language in which we articulate our experiences and the meanings life has for us. Stories are, then, a way of knowing and sharing with others what we know and a way for others to share with us what they know.

In this book we suggest that the *workplace* contains a vast array of stories—life stories, work stories, interpersonal and group stories, leaders' stories, and our stories about the organization and its leaders. This book explores these stories for understanding and meaning. The stories we are about to tell explore two fundamental questions: How did things go at work today? What is it like to work here? The answers to these questions point to an underappreciated complexity in workplace experience and also to the darker side of our lives at work.

The workplace stories we tell say a lot about human nature, stress and strains, and coping with anxiety, all of which may evoke psychologically

3

defensive responses in order to cope with distressing workplace experience. In particular, in organizations much of human nature is expressed through what leaders and followers do in their relationships with one another. This doing may be wonderful and humane or devolve into abusive, manipulative, and sadistic behavior that is harmful to everyone in the workplace, sabotaging the organization's ability to perform well enough to adapt and survive in the marketplace.

By focusing on the dark side of human nature, this book is about toxic workplaces, as seen and heard through the medium of stories and storytelling. It is also a book about storytelling as an approach to knowing and healing organizations and people. We will argue that storytelling is a crucial component of studying and working with organizations, a vital qualitative method to help understand and explain organizational life, and a way to facilitate humane change. Storytelling helps to affirm the humanity of people in workplaces and helps people and groups to heal. Further, storytelling offers access to the breadth and depth of workplace experience, what Michael Diamond (1993) calls the unconscious life of organizations, a world ruled more by the irrational dark side of human nature than by rationality and enlightened self-interest.

Why Organizational Stories and Storytelling?

Using stories from the workplace raises important questions. Why should stories count as organizational data? Why has an interest in stories and storytelling burgeoned since the early 1990s? What do stories offer organizational research and consulting that traditional quantitative data do not? Yiannis Gabriel, an international authority on stories and storytelling, writes that "stories are pithy narratives with plots, characters and twists that can be full of meaning. Successful stories have beginnings, middles and ends" (Gabriel, 2011).

The core of stories is meaning and experience. Stories matter because they help us make sense of our experiences. They enable us to learn from the experiences of other people. Stories express our emotions and can trigger change or become stumbling blocks to change. Stories are vital ways in which we construct our individual and group identities and sustain our bonds to our communities and places of work (Gabriel, 2011).

Since the 1990s stories and storytelling have blossomed in social science research. *People hunger for stories.* Stories offer affective (emotional), expressive, and symbolic dimensions of life and are not limited to the instrumental or practical. Gabriel writes that "research on organizational storytelling accelerated considerably since the 1990's when stories started to make regular appearances as 'data' for organizational analysis" (Gabriel, 2011). Data collection now often includes stories. For example, Stein wrote two early books based largely on clinical stories and stories from health-care organizations: *Clinical Stories and Their Translations* (with Maurice Apprey, 1990) and *Listening Deeply* (1994). Both Stein and Allcorn, together with Howell Baum and Michael Diamond, wrote *The Human Cost of a Management Failure: Downsizing at General Hospital* (1996), which tells the story of what happened at this hospital through the voices of more than twenty hospital executives whom we interviewed three times in one year.

Gabriel addresses the timing or context of renewed interest in stories:

Why do stories influence hearts and minds in a way that the cold power of logic, science and facts fail to do? It seems to me that the ready availability of information and data, far from undermining the power of storytelling, has reinforced it. In a world where many of us are choking in information and data, facts, figures and PowerPoint slides, stories cut through and communicate meaning with remarkable speed and economy. If we have a professional problem or a management problem we will often turn to a person who has experienced and managed to overcome a similar problem, seeking to learn from their experience. (Gabriel, 2011)

In the stories that follow, we will suggest that just as dreams are a way to understand the individual unconscious, stories—like folklore and myth in preliterate society—are a way to understand the unconscious as well as well as the conscious dimensions of experience and meaning in organizational life. In fact the stories of our lives at work are a route to knowing the workplace and our experience of it. Further, stories and storytelling are an approach to both knowing and healing organizations and people. Stories are, then, a way of knowing organizational life in greater depth, offering rich opportunities for meaningful change.

Some Other Perspectives on Storytelling

Before proceeding further, we would like to note alternate, nonpsychodynamic ways of thinking about stories and storytelling that are drawn from business and organizational perspectives and beyond. Stories and storytelling are used in many ways in organizations, and the history of doing so is long. Storytelling is one of the foundations of managing public relations and marketing, and it is often used in branding the company and its products and services. Becoming effective at crafting a narrative is the subject of much discussion on the Internet, where many helpful suggestions are provided to improve this important task. In telling our stories in this book, we are using them for a much different purpose. We tell the stories to encourage readers to explore and reflect upon the often dark side of the workplace and their own experiences.

Stories in the management literature are also helpful in leading and managing organizations (Smith, 2012). Stories in many forms, such as stories about organizational history, as well as stories about what recently happened, can help to promote understanding, integration, and mutual sharing of experience, as well as a shared sense of the organizational narrative and culture (Armstrong, 1992; James & Minnis, 2004). Organization members can in effect join a narrative as they come together to collectively create and then listen to it, pass it on to others, and experience it daily in their work. Leaders and managers effectively use stories to paint a picture and frame conversations about events, work, and problem solving—stories that often become the party line, or obligatory myth. Stories can be important in terms of promoting learning about basic concepts and principles that help organizational members become more effective and work more safely. For example, stories about injuries at work are sobering and cautionary, and people who have not heard them may be doomed to be injured themselves. Our stories also serve in part to promote understanding, as well as the critical thinking and reflectivity not always encouraged by management.

Stories can also inspire and motivate organization members to strive for higher performance standards, increased productivity, and greater efficiency. Workplaces always have stories about big bonuses for a successful year and layoffs during bad years. The charismatic CEO and senior leaders may also provide motivational stories that address vision and mission. Organizational meetings may include invited guests who tell inspirational stories about how a product or service might have saved a life or provided an exceptionally good experience. An example of this might be a mother telling a story to a gathering of trauma center managers and supervisors about how their work in one hospital saved her child's life.

Stories have many intentional uses: to promote products, services, organizations, and leaders, perhaps with the aim of manipulating what others think and feel and do. That is the goal of marketing. Management can also purposefully use stories to convey to employees a sense of organizational culture, an overarching vision of the organization, and a sense of belonging to something important.

Of course not all stories in the workplace are created and managed by leaders. The grapevine, the rumor mill, and chats in the lunch room and at the water fountain exemplify this aspect of organizational life, where the stories may not be consistent with how management wants stories used and are beyond the reach of management to control. In these informal settings organizational events may be redefined and interpreted, in turn exposing a darker and more ominous side to what is taking place than the stories created by management. Once again we note that the stories we will tell in this book are not intended to serve these management purposes but rather to illuminate the dark side of organizational life that we then hold up for reflection, inspection, discussion, and analysis with psychodynamically informed perspectives (Hummel, 1991; Pollack & Bono, 2013).

Stories and storytelling are hardly limited to business and organizational environments. Stories and storytelling have been central to the human saga since the development of language. They pervade human history and culture. From American Indians to sub-Saharan Africans to Slavic and Latino Americans, hunter-gatherer bands, tribes, and ethnic groups have used storytelling for multiple purposes. Stories and storytelling are used (1) to convey group identity—who we are and how we came to be (origin myths); (2) to transmit history through myth and folklore; (3) to share knowledge about the world and how to make one's way in it; (4) to offer moral lessons and guidance; and (5) to explain customs. Oral traditions long preceded, and everywhere now continue side by side with, written traditions.

People convey and construct their narrative history through stories. Storytelling is perhaps the essence of the mass media. From the Internet to movies storytelling is also entertainment. Museum collections and displays tell the stories the curators wish to tell in anticipation of what they think patrons wish to see. Social networking also provides for storytelling that is transnational and multicultural. Finally, Michael White and David Epton (1990) founded a school for, and devised a method of, narrative family therapy. They help people to externalize and reflect upon internal experience and then to craft new stories—precisely our method and goal in this book about organizational life. We turn now to the exploration through stories of unconscious processes in the workplace, which is the focus of this book.

A Reflection on Us (All)

In this book we explore persecutory, frightening, and just plain nasty organizational events through stories. People engage in a never-ending effort to make some sense of this side of life by telling stories about it. And these distressing experiences from the workplace often seem to be never ending, with one abuse followed by another.

At the same time it is only human to turn away from what is too horrible to hear and observe. This may in fact make it a challenge for the reader to absorb the stories in this book. The stories are, however, there—like it or not. Denial, rationalization, and turning away lead to the inability to learn from experience, and without learning and reflection there is no change. Life at work will not get better if it is not open to inspection.

Many stories in this book are based on our firsthand experiences, while we observed others, and still others were reported to us. We have modified them for reasons of confidentiality. At the same time the integrity of the stories remains intact. All the stories that we offer actually happened in organizations, and they happened to real people.

The majority of these stories happened to us, the authors, either as actors or observers or both, during our forty-five-year careers. There is, then, an autobiographical orientation in telling the stories. These stories, events, and happenings shaped our lives at work. In many instances they evoked disbelief and generated an enduring drive to try to understand and appreciate *why* the events in these stories happened to us or to those around us. It is also important to appreciate that we did not pass through all this workplace experience and terrain without its having significant effects on our personal and psychological well-being. No one can say events like these do not create fear, anxiety, suffering, and financial loss. Being personally attacked and bullied across months and years at work is ultimately a soul-stripping experience. We acknowledge this. We have experienced it. We are saying that it is okay to feel the hurt, fear, and anger. You are not alone in this experience.

The stories provided here offer an opportunity to take a time-out from workplace and organizational experience. They hold organizational events up for inspection. In particular this inspection process reveals that, while the stories and voices are all different, they are also much the same. They share much in terms of content and themes.

An important first step is acknowledging that the telling of the stories offers at least a partial way out of the swamp of personal distress and despair. When others read and listen and perhaps validate the stories and experience in this book—"Yes, this also happened to me"—they may gain a sense of being emotionally held and comforted for a moment (Goodman & Meyers, 2012). "I understand you." Storytelling is, then, for us as authors and for you as readers, a contribution to restoring a sense of well-being, wholeness, and personal integrity. "I survived. And I *learned* in the process of surviving." Hearing our stories and telling your stories is a way out of the swamp to a higher ground, where some sense of personal healing may occur.

Some Overarching Themes

The stories we relate in the chapters that follow can stand alone as interesting in and of themselves. They can also be embedded in larger overarching or underlying stories—for example, about the United States and even more broadly about human nature as it is expressed in organizational life. This perspective does not change the content of the stories. Rather it puts a large frame around the stories and thereby gives them broader and deeper meaning.

Theme One

Our first overarching theme is that "you couldn't make this up," something we said to each other and ourselves as reassurance that the stories actually happened. In its own way each story is emotionally counterintuitive. It is difficult, if not impossible, to imagine how irrational the professional workplace is. Thus these stories are outside the boundary of ordinary stories or narratives of American culture. The workplace stories strike us as bizarre, absurd, even irrational. What rational organization, for instance, throws away millions of dollars in income to feed the narcissistic appetite of its leader?

Our widely shared American fantasy about rationality in economics, politics, and decision making has no space for stories such as these. "That's impossible," "it did not or could not have happened," and "it violates common sense!" are common reactions and protests to stories like these. "People don't destroy their own organizations! They maximize productivity, profit, shareholder value, and efficiency!" Right? Denial is a powerful psychological defense.

In our widely shared ideal cultural self-image, we like to think of ourselves as rational, objective, grounded in reality, kindly, compassionate, and driven economically toward greater efficiency, productivity, and profit. The stories offered in this book present an alternate view of organizational life, identity, function, and outcome. The stories mirror the dark side of ourselves in our myriad for-profit, public, and nonprofit organizations.

Part of our purpose in gathering and telling these stories is to turn the impossible into the possible, to make the unimaginable imaginable. The stories bring dark secrets and taboos into the daylight of thought and reflection. When we learned or experienced these stories, we had to overcome our own resistance to acknowledging that this really happened. For us the challenge was, and is, to move these stories from the realm of impossibility to possibility and with that to reality.

Idealized cultural models such as rational man, objectivity, and enlightened self-interest are often not reality. Ultimately to take these stories seriously is to alter our perception, definition, and experience of *reality* itself. It requires that we overcome our own resistance and believe the unbelievable. In turn it requires that we relinquish a cherished ideal image about what organizational reality is like. This letting go triggers a sense of disorientation and anxiety about a lost and comforting ideal. If we can allow ourselves to suspend belief in these models, perhaps the emotionally indigestible may become digestible. That is, we may be more able to acknowledge that this really happens at work.

Theme Two

A second overarching theme unites many of these stories: Stories do not exist as entities by themselves. Stories always emerge from a relationship between storyteller and listener. We, the authors, learned that we had a specific kind of relationship with the people who told some of these stories to us. We became witnesses. We did not simply collect data called workplace stories. What we were given was more like a gift of knowledge and insight offered in trust by those who told us their stories. In retelling these stories we are bearing witness: "Yes, this actually happened."

Many people thanked us for listening. No one had been interested in their experience. We might add that the poet Carolyn Forché identified an entire genre she called a "poetry of witness." Ours might be thought of as organizational stories of witness. Paradoxically the secret that must not be acknowledged or uttered is known by virtually everyone—what Christopher Bollas (1989) called the "unthought known." The act of witnessing the telling of a workplace story permits the storyteller to throw off the shroud of secrecy that had made the story so oppressive and life destroying. In storytelling both storyteller and listener witness the trauma—the injury to the self and the suffering that is a consequence of the injury. In the presence of the listener, the storyteller can give symbolic shape to unspeakable experience.

On one occasion one of us interviewed a female executive about her experience of organizational downsizing. At the conclusion of the interview he asked her how she felt about the interview. She paused and said, "I came in with a migraine headache. Now it's gone." The act of being listened to had apparently had a therapeutic and healing effect. Inseparable from her storytelling was the listener's witnessing her telling of her experience. We can surmise in retrospect that what often occurred was that the listener served as a container (Bion, 1962) for the interviewee's story and anxiety and as a "holding environment" (Winnicott, 1965) in which a person feels psychologically held by the interviewer, consultant, or therapist in an emotionally safe place.

Theme Three

Yet a third underlying theme is part of the fabric of all these individual and varied stories. While at one level each story is unique, at a deeper level many stories are embedded in the culture of the United States and the

American workplace, and they express the darker side of human nature. These individual stories become embodiments of both American culture and of the universality of human unconscious dynamics. We suggest the themes of these stories also apply to other countries and cultures. Human nature is universal and one of the major driving forces in the stories shared here. At the same time the organizational context (hierarchical, corporate, public sector) of these stories is increasingly common around the world. Life at work is global, as are human nature and organizations.

Theme Four

A fourth overarching theme is the sheer power of leaders. The stories suggest that leaders can infect lower-echelon executives, managers, and workers with the leaders' pathological tendencies. At the same time management by intimidation co-opts members of the organization into tacitly enabling what the leader does, including unethical and illegal behavior. Messengers are sacrificed and whistleblowers are destroyed. Losing one's job is not a good option. Leaders have the power to hire and fire. You have to get with the program, join the team, and dutifully submit to authority—or look for a new job. We suggest dominance and submission are part of the uncomfortable reality of the workplace.

Theme Five

One final theme is not prominent in our stories: the *brighter* side of organizational life. Human resilience, organizational resilience, the resilience of the human spirit, and the determination to survive are also stories about the workplace. We, and those who told us the stories, have in fact lived to tell them. We did survive. Although religion has appropriated the human spirit for its own purposes, that spirit also exists independently in secular forms and settings such as workplaces. What might be called secular spirituality is another way of understanding the workplace and the ability of people and organizations to survive the worst dysfunctions (Allcorn, 2002).

Individual (and organizational) plasticity helps people to adapt to the worst of circumstances and in many instances to survive and even prevail. Some of what we have gleaned from our stories hints at how this might be possible: listening to others from the heart as well as the head; validating people's experiences; listening that is witnessing and affirming, so that people will not be condemned to be alone in their experience and suffering. One's spirit may be harmed by others and organizational events, but it may also be observed to be indomitable.

The Lessons to Be Learned

As we have already noted, the stories and discussions here peel back the fantasized layers of rationality that are presumed to govern the workplace and reveal the irrationality of the darker side of organizational life. The stories consistently remind us of things that happen that are bad for employees and bad for organizations. Bad things happen, and, as we have said, you could never imagine they could happen. Acknowledging these aspects of life at work—including the daily frictions we all experience relative to each other and to accomplishing work, as well as management-created dysfunctions and at times sweeping devastation—is the necessary first step to finding a better and more enlightened workplace experience that enhances organizational performance and experience.

The workplace stories provided here lead us to consider what can be done and whether it has to be like this. The answer, we firmly believe, is *no*. No, it does not have to be this way. However, achieving this will take a national commitment by boards of directors, CEOs, senior executives, managers, and employees to acknowledge the less-than-rational nature of the workplace, which in turn makes it safe to spot the stories as they unfold and find ways to intervene before they do damage. We explore this further in the concluding chapters of this book.

We Are Not Alone

As we have noted, the stories at the core of this book come largely from the dark side of the workplace, where individual and organizational dysfunction and toxicity exist. These arise from a broad array of human and group behaviors that are often driven by unconscious and irrational dynamics. That many, if not most, of the stories feel unbelievable, especially in juxtaposition with the image of a presumably rational, organized, and planned workplace, has not gone unnoticed by many organizational researchers and psychodynamically informed authors. Many of these authors have clinical backgrounds but not all do. In this section it is not our intention to provide a comprehensive or even a modest review of this ever-growing literature and approach to understanding life at work. Rather, we select a few writers whom we consider representative of the contribution made by psychoanalytically informed theory and organizational diagnosis. Their approaches complement each other.

Manfred Kets de Vries has published many books that offer insight into this irrational and largely unconscious side of the workplace. In *The Leader on the Couch* (2006), he provides many clinically and psychodynamically informed insights into the unconscious side of organizational life. He writes,

> A psychologically informed perspective can help us understand the hidden dynamics associated with individual motivation, leadership, collusive situations, social defenses, toxic organizational cultures, "neurotic" organizations (that is organizations tainted by the particular neurosis of its top executive), and the extent to which individuals and organizations can be prisoners of their past. (Kets de Vries, 2006, p. 7)

In this single sentence he lays out many possibilities for understanding individual and organizational dynamics.

Specifically an ever-present tension exists between the conscious and unconscious dimensions of individuals and groups in relation to the leadership styles of CEOs and other senior-level executives, who have power that cannot always or even often be mitigated by group dynamics, at least in the United States. Further, groups in the workplace, whether they are formal divisions or subsections or informal groupings or project-based temporary arrangements, contain leaders and followers and produce interactions that possess unconscious elements that often produce irrationality and toxic behaviors. Some of these dynamics may defend against hard-to-discuss workplace anxieties that may result from the top-down actions of CEOs and senior executives. These leaders may well permeate their organizations with their own unconscious and irrational thoughts, feelings, and actions.

Our workplace stories provide concrete real-life examples of the darker side of conscious and unconscious thoughts and feelings. The stories point out personally and organizationally destructive workplace behavior by powerful leaders and members of work groups. We agree with Kets de Vries that to understand the events in the stories, one must turn to psychology.

In *The Unconscious Life of Organizations* (1993) Michael Diamond uses organizational identity as an instrument for understanding the presence of unconscious workplace behavior. People join organizations, stay in organizations, and change organizations for both conscious and unconscious reasons. Organizational identity speaks to these myriad conscious and unconscious individual and group dynamics within the workplace. Diamond defines organizational identity as

the totality of repetitive patterns of individual behavior and interpersonal relationship that, when taken together, comprise the unacknowledged meaning of organizational life. Organization identity is influenced by conscious thought; however, its relational patterns among individuals at work are primarily motivated by unconscious thoughts and feelings. Its foundation rests with the transference of emotions beneath organizational structure. (Diamond, 1993, p. 77)

For Diamond the essence of organizational identity is the quality of emotional attachments, connectedness, and mutual understanding, or lack thereof, that exists in all groups and organizations. The nature of the intersubjectivity (unconscious communication between people) between superiors and subordinates, as well as among all organizational participants, is another way of describing this essence. How we see ourselves, each other, the groups that we participate in, and our organizations is filled with unconscious elements of feeling nurtured or dominated and abused. Organizational identity therefore directs our attention to who we are as a group and organization. This arises in part consciously (vision, mission, values statements, and strategic plans) and from the network of unconscious individual and shared interpersonal strategies for coping with and defending against actual or perceived stress in the workplace.

The workplace stories shared in this book illustrate the many ways to understand organizational life and identity. Notably the darker side of human nature profoundly permeates who I am, who you are, and who we are in the stories. This in turn is energized by unconscious thoughts and feelings that are enacted, often repetitively, without much reflection. In many ways the resulting behaviors in the stories defy logical understanding. They are ultimately filled with irrationality.

Yiannis Gabriel, in *Organizations in Depth* (1999), begins by noting that, on the surface, organizations appear ordinary, stable, and to be doing work and business in ways that make good sense. He then argues that

> the psychoanalytic conception of organizations goes far beyond the examination of the pathological and unusual. Psychoanalysis can provide a deep understanding of many features of organizations, even those that appear perfectly straightforward and ordinary. It does this by examining not so much the behavior of individuals in organizations, but rather the *meaning* of their behavior and the deeper *motives* for the actions. (Gabriel, 1999, p. 1)

Gabriel is suggesting that psychoanalytically informed perspectives can contribute to understanding organizational life. The workplace is filled with individuals who often act, think, and feel based on less than fully conscious desires and wishes. The presence of unusual pathological individuals and exceptionally hard-to-believe organizational events encourages the inspection of the workplace from a psychodynamically informed perspective. This appreciation underscores the growing necessity to understand organizations using organizational theory to examine human behavior in large public spaces and the intimate internal nature of private space (Gabriel, 1999).

Our workplace stories include a sense of meaning grounded in the deeper motivations of the events and protagonists. The story written on a page helps to create a visual scenario of this meaning. Then, following the story, a psychoanalytically informed discussion and analysis opens the door to appreciating some, if not many, of the unconscious motivations of behavior that are difficult to tolerate relative to oneself and others. We hope the stories make the hard-to-believe side of workplace experience real and filled with meaning and significance.

In *The Psychodynamics of Work and Organizations* (1993), William Czander begins by duly noting that hierarchical modern organizations

have accomplished much that is good and positive in the service of progress. Further, many theorists and teachers, he notes, hope for a newer and
better way to structure organizations that will give rise to increased commitment and spirit. Regarding contemporary organizations, he writes,
"Invariably they come up short. Perhaps the reason is their lack of understanding of the conscious and unconscious forces that bind people
together and stimulate motivations for work and achievement, or perhaps they do not adequately understand the 'dark' forces that underlie
human behavior, or they fail to understand what Fromm (1970) refers
to as 'system man'" (Czander, 1993, p. 1). System men (and women) are
individuals who are angry, alienated, and unhappy at work yet are willing
to conform. These people abandon a sense of control over their lives in
return for money that allows them to compensate for this loss of positive
self-experience by acquiring material goods. Czander notes,

> From a psychoanalytic perspective, attachment to work is consid-
> ered the result of the gratification of conscious and unconscious fan-
> tasies associated with occupational and career aspirations. It is the
> content of these fantasies and their analysis that provides insights
> into how the organization can change, and increases the probability
> of gratification associated with work. (Czander, 1993, p.7)

Ultimately organizations fail to fulfill these compensatory fantasies of
self-fulfillment that often arise from early family-related narcissistic injuries or other psychological injuries that occur throughout adult life.
Organization members unconsciously seek to fulfill these fantasies,
sometimes compulsively. This effort is in part continually frustrated by
the nature of hierarchical organizations, which offer limited numbers of
higher-level positions that might be able to fulfill these deeply felt personal needs. Further, organizations essentially use people to make a profit—and in the twenty-first century do so without much commitment to
employee well-being.

In this book our stories take place in bureaucratic hierarchies in which
individuals with virtually unlimited power and authority at the top of
the pyramid act unilaterally relative to all the employees below them. The
stories illustrate that much of what happens within our supposedly ratio-

nally designed and operated hierarchical organizations is not so rational at all. Exceptional harm can be done to individuals and paradoxically also to organizational performance. Employees often will say that they like their work, such as caring for others. They may also say that they like most of the people they work with, sometimes making lifelong friends. But they also often say that they hate their job, indicating a disdain for how they are managed—usually in a top-down manner—and how the organization is managed in general. Fulfilling personal needs at work is therefore problematic and most often not seen as the goal of organizations.

In sum these four representative authors offer psychodynamically informed insights about people and groups at work, leaders and followers, the nature of organizational design, and the omnipresence of unconscious motivations for thoughts, feelings, and actions at work. The many different faces of human nature, combined in a mix of large numbers of employees who work within a traditional organizational hierarchy, introduce ever-changing complexity. In turn this complexity results sometimes in outstanding individual and organizational performance and humanism, and at other times in the introduction of dysfunctional and, many would say, pathological, intrapersonal, interpersonal, group, and organizational dynamics that are represented in some form in our stories about the workplace.

Organization of This Book

Our approach, or method, is simple. Chapters 2 and 3 orient work and workers within theory and practice. Chapter 2 underscores the need for a research method and approach for understanding the significant contribution that irrationality makes to workplace dynamics—some good and some dark in nature. Chapter 3 explains our use of terminology drawn from psychoanalytic theory by providing accessible definitions, accompanied by stories of how the terms relate to life at work. Starting with part 2 we introduce four chapters of stories. Each story consists of three parts: the story, or "case," itself, followed by questions designed to encourage readers to take a moment to reflect on the story and their own life experiences at work that may be similar, and a discussion and analysis that explores the psychodynamics embedded in the story. The third part is similar to the remark the editorialist Paul Harvey used to sign off his radio broadcasts: "And now you know the rest of the story." These stories often lead to the conclusion that experiences at work can be stranger than fiction.

We now offer a word about how we have organized the chapters. The stories are arranged in groups around themes, all of which illustrate different facets of organizational darkness. Chapter 4 includes stories about dysfunctional and toxic leadership. Chapter 5 includes stories about the interactions that arise between leaders and followers that involve unconscious dynamics that influence how leaders and followers see each other and themselves. Chapter 6 explores some of the many faces of organizational toxicity and dysfunction by providing an array of stories that underscore the complexity of truly understanding the workplace. Chapter 7 provides stories that link physical or spatial aspects of the workplace, such as furniture, offices, and buildings, to what are sometimes painful memories and the uses of these physical aspects as symbols of power as well as narcissistic aggrandizement. Part 3 provides two concluding chapters. In chapter 8 we look back upon the stories to find the tale they tell about the contemporary workplace—the light side and the dark side. What in particular do the themes of the stories tell us, and what sense can we make of their cumulative tale? Chapter 9 concludes the book by looking forward in terms of exploring the future of the workplace and in particular how a psychodynamically informed perspective provides insights necessary for understanding the irrational nature of our lives at work.

We begin our journey into organizational darkness with a discussion of how a psychoanalytic perspective can help us to understand organizations in ways that elude more conventional empirical approaches.

CHAPTER 2

Why Use a Psychoanalytic Approach to Understand Organizations?

Business literature has explored many theoretical perspectives. In general these authors do not provide in-depth psychological explorations of the workplace, especially examinations that use psychoanalytic theory. At best many authors cite or provide research using quantitative methods, or they advocate rational approaches to work that fall short of explaining why an individual or group did what it did. Books such as *Reasoning, Learning and Action* (1983) by Chris Argyris; *Organizational Culture and Leadership* (2010) by Edgar Schein; or *Bad Leadership* (2004) by Barbara Kellerman are examples. These books delve into the less-than-logical, and even darker, side of human nature without deeply exploring the psychodynamics that underpin the behavior. From our perspective these books therefore are incomplete at best and many times do not represent what actually goes on at work.

Let us briefly highlight the differences. Argyris (1983) assumes that rationality is possible if employees systematically examine their lives at work and the workplace. This assumption largely ignores the many irrational and unconscious psychodynamics that are omnipresent in organizations (Diamond, 1986). While Schein (2010) occasionally acknowledges the presence of psychodynamics in the workplace, he does not firmly embrace the implications of this reality, preferring instead to focus on having presumably rational executives design and redesign organizational culture by manipulating underlying principles and values.

They adopt what works and discard the rest in what Schein implies is a logical process. And while Kellerman clearly acknowledges and explores the dark side of leadership and followership in organizations, she largely ignores the contributions that a psychodynamically informed perspective could make to understanding the bad leadership typology she describes. This typology includes incompetent, rigid, intemperate, callous, corrupt, insular, and evil individuals (Kellerman, 2004). Most readers would expect that people who act this way have emotional issues that the author would explain with a psychodynamic exploration of this typology, but the book provides nothing along these lines.

A vast amount of research and theorizing of this nature often points out unusual and dysfunctional behavior in the workplace but invariably does not illuminate the unconscious and irrational processes at work, preferring instead the creation of typologies and prescriptions that rely on rationality. We now turn to our effort to remediate this problem.

We begin this chapter by embracing only one assumption: *All organizations, large or small, public or private, share one thing in common—people, people who imagine these organizations, create them, and operate them.* Human nature is therefore a pervasive influence in organizations and has both rational and irrational elements. Understanding both sides is essential to understanding individual, interpersonal, group, and organizational dynamics.

Rationality and Organizations

Rationality is what we expect in and from organizations and the groups and individuals who staff them. Mission, goals, and objectives should be published only after careful consideration, and the methods, tactics, and processes used to fulfill them ideally should be designed with engineering and mathematical precision to achieve cost effectiveness and delivery of quality-assured products on time and under budget. In a highly competitive world marketplace failure is not a good option. Success, these books say, is assured by pursuing rationality in all things, including even our personal lives. Used in a business sense the expression "Ready, aim, fire" emphasizes this careful attention to rationality.

Supposed rationality in the workplace invariably rests upon the presumption that the underlying elements of bureaucratic, hierarchical structure are rational, that is, that the organization's vertical layers of positions have systematic coordination built into their design. Added to the hierarchy are usually the development and enforcement of rules and regulations, policies and procedures, and engineered designs of such things as business processes and assembly lines. Ideally virtually no aspect of an organization and its operations is ignored in the twenty-first century. "If you cannot measure it, you cannot manage it" is an aphorism based on the notion of scientific management popularized by Frederick W. Taylor in the early twentieth century. According to this model, every aspect of the workplace should be examined for its contribution to the bottom line. "No margin, no mission" is a common slogan. These books put a premium on Six Sigma Black Belts—process and quality-control managers who rely on empirical and statistical methods—as well as on CEOs who make the numbers. Edgar Schein (2010) advocates managing even the soft side of organizations, their culture.

But Does It Work?

Methods, processes, and policies and procedures can be subjected to continuous improvement and occasionally reengineered or transformed to meet new challenges and fulfill new opportunities for optimization and adaptation. In fact legions of consultants, academics, and researchers continually advocate this work, especially if they are hired to help the organization or want to sell books. The possibilities are limitless.

However, accurate reality testing frequently points out that organizations fail for reasons too numerous to outline here. We suggest that what they all share are lapses in rationality, and the examples comprise a pantheon of huge corporate names—General Motors, Enron, Bear Sterns, Lehman Brothers, WorldCom, Washington Mutual, AIG, CITI, Conseco, Chrysler, the Time-Warner merger, and Pacific Gas and Electric—as well as such bankrupt cities as Vallejo and San Bernardino, California, and Detroit. Some would say that these massive failures are the result of losses of rationality and not the fault of rationality as an organizing principle. Then how did this happen? We suggest that, while rationality has easily recognized limitations such as the limits of perfect knowledge, the people involved ultimately failed to act rationally—from the CEO all the way down to the lowest levels of the hierarchy. It seems that failure is all too often an option, one promoted by an unquestioned and some-times ideological belief in rationality. People do not always do the logical thing. Optimizing an illogical system does not always or often improve its performance.

Irrationality and Organizations

If we embrace the reality that organizations are created and operated by fallible humans, we are much better able to appreciate why organization-al life sometimes does not make much sense. While on the surface orga-nizations appear to embrace a model of mathematical precision, much like a clock, they are permeated at all levels by irrational, individual, in-terpersonal, group, and organizational dynamics. Understanding these dynamics is essential but also is much more challenging than determin-ing how to optimize an assembly line, a supply chain, financing, or a marketing program.

The following point is worth noting at the outset: Based on our decades of executive and consulting experience, we contend that the idea that ex-ecutives and managers systematically manage by the numbers is simply not true. It is often painfully easy to observe that key data elements about production processes are not collected or, if they are, that the actual data are not clearly defined or systematically collected, resulting in data whose integrity is compromised. All these problematic data are then rolled up into reports and analyses that often include false assumptions, data cal-culation errors, and self-protective distortions of information. Eventu-ally reality is largely lost by the time information reaches the top of the organization.

In sum, rational by-the-numbers management is often not at all ratio-nal. In saying this we are not relying exclusively on the distorting effects of human nature to hide, conceal, change, and recast data and events for defensive self-serving purposes. Rather we point to poorly conceived data collection and manipulation, improperly prepared reporting formats, and pressure to continually simplify reports. These are in turn often driv-en by fads and aggravated by constant turnover among those collecting, manipulating, reporting, and using the information and reports. In fact one can most often find potentially knowable information buried in un-representative, untimely, and poorly analyzed data. While these losses of knowledge certainly include among their causes psychologically defensive processes, they are often simply the result of poorly conceived and operated management information systems. In this regard management is not so much irrational at times as it is nonrational, in the sense that managers could have good information, but they paradoxically expend little or no effort to get it. However, in many instances the irrational exerts a much greater influence over what is already an irrational faith in the rational workplace.

Is the workplace filled with the irrationalities that accompany human nature? Yes, it is. Is it easy to see irrational forces at play everywhere, all the time, in the workplace? Yes, it is. Is it the case most of the time that the toughest problems to solve are personnel problems? Yes, it is. Is it easy to find instances of arrogance, vindictiveness, backstabbing, and intense pursuit of self-interest to the exclusion of benefiting the organization, as well as aggression, bullying, discrimination of all kinds, and hard-to-believe decisions and actions that in hindsight produced highly detrimental outcomes? Yes, it is. During a short chat over coffee with a seasoned silver-haired management consultant, we asked, "How many well-managed companies have you encountered?" After a few moments of reflection the response was "Only one."

The stories we offer in this book make it clear that the workplace is filled with irrationality; psychologically defensive thoughts, feelings, and actions; and destructive interpersonal, group, and organizational behavior. Most often it seems the only way to make this clear is by telling stories. "Did you hear what they did?" "Guess what happened yesterday." At times the workplace can seem like a good novel or movie—and the novel or movie can seem like a workplace.

If it is reasonable and even rational to accept that the workplace is filled with irrationalities, then how does one go about understanding this side of work life? We suggest the best way to understand the underlying dynamics is to use what has been learned about psychology since the early twentieth century, in particular an understanding based on psychoanalytically informed theory that strives to understand human development and nature in a way that reveals the humanity and fragility within human nature. Understanding why a CEO or executive is willing to expend almost any amount of time and energy to control and dominate senior management, and sometimes lower-level employees, is a challenge that can be met only by gaining a psychodynamically informed insight into the individual, group, and organizational dynamics. Chapter 3 further illuminates how psychoanalytically informed theory can readily be used to understand human behavior in the workplace.

Conclusion: The Workplace—Rational and Irrational

We have made two points. The workplace contains many rational elements in terms of how the organization is structured, how it is led and managed, and how work is designed, sometimes down to microscopic levels. This is what such ideas as scientific management and management engineering are about. But many things happen at work that are not so logical. Decisions are often made based on untimely, distorted, and incomplete information that may produce hard-to-believe and unintended outcomes, as well as disasters that kill people. The ostensibly rational workplace is often not firmly grounded in accurate reality testing. Certainly management information systems can have built-in deficiencies and flaws that compromise the idea of rational decision making, implementation, and ongoing management. Nonrationality does exist and exerts powerful consequences on organizational productivity, profitability, and morale.

Nonrationality notwithstanding, we tell stories to illustrate that the workplace is also filled with irrationality. For example, a CEO who has been given clear, timely, and well-analyzed information that a decision he made a year ago produced major financial losses might choose to ignore the information and suppress it from public and internal review in order to maintain his reputation as a great leader. He asserts that the blame for the outcome lies not with his conception and design of the project but rather with all those who were responsible for implementing it. The US invasion of Iraq in 2003 with too few forces and the resulting chaos were not viewed by those at the top of the U.S. government as the result of flawed thinking but rather as a problem with how the invasion was carried out on the ground. Flower petals welcoming the invading forces were nowhere to be seen; the financial costs were not minimal; and no evidence of an impending mushroom cloud was found. Policy makers who conceived the project never acknowledged their mistakes.

Psychoanalytic Insight and Wisdom: The Why of Organizational Life

Our stories from the workplace draw attention to many confounding and complex aspects of our experiences at work. In particular such understanding is often a matter of knowing—as basic journalism requires—who, what, where, when, and why. However, the *why* part of this recipe often eludes our ability to know and explain. Why did they think, feel, and do this? What led a group to such inexplicable and unrealistic decisions and action? Why did an organization of people end up doing what they did—good or bad? The stories in this book begin to address these questions. The stories point to the conclusion that the bizarre and often irrational parts of our workplace experience can become a dominating force in people's lives at work.

These stories from the workplace raise unavoidable interest in and concern for the powerful influence of human nature on every aspect of an organization, including employees, who create the organization every day they come to work. Throughout history human nature has led to many admired and wonderful acts of support and kindness for others and groups. These daily caretaking actions by many in the workplace are generous and should be acknowledged and nurtured. They are part of work life that people report when they say they like their work and the people with whom they work.

In contrast the darker side of human nature introduces commonly found organizational processes that may be described as sadistic, brutal, unnecessary, regrettable, harmful, self-destructive, dysfunctional, mean, aggressive, abusive, and impersonal ("nothing personal, just business") (Stein, 2001). Regrettably these descriptions reflect what it is like to work here, what the culture and identity of the workplace are. Their effects on our experience, the experience of others, and the workplace itself most often dwarf those facets of the workplace that express the humane and uplifting side of human nature. Understanding why these things happen requires peering into the dark side of human nature with a psychodynamically informed perspective in order to make sense of the events or at least appreciate the nonsense and irrationality (Adams & Balfour, 2009).

Sense Making and Detoxification

The stories in this book are the product of relationships: between one of us and someone else, both of us with others, and as an ongoing conversation between the two of us. Our conversations with other people, and with each other, consisted of making sense of what we had experienced and heard. This began to detoxify the emotional content of the stories. The stories were in themselves a step toward personal validation and healing. The people who told us their stories and we ourselves often felt alone, isolated, crazy, unable to make sense of and digest what we had experienced. An abusive experience often makes the victim feel immobilized, paralyzed, unable either to be rid of it or to make it past tense. Abuse freezes the victim in time and space. The stories speak to the experience of feeling dirty, polluted, defiled, icky, and nauseated by the workplace. This harm may take many forms, but in all cases it diminishes us as human beings.

The process of relating stories to other people, and of making sense of the stories with another person, is profoundly validating. The process helps to detoxify what the employee has experienced as emotionally invasive and poisonous. It helps others—and us—to be able to digest and metabolize what the employee has experienced. This hoped-for outcome can be transformative and, in psychoanalytic terms, change this internalized experience (bad object) into something less threatening and dominating. Telling our and your stories to others makes the content of the experience less unthinkable and more tolerable to think about and feel. This appreciation emerges while reading the workplace stories told here.

As we shall explore, storytelling has a preventive dimension in addition to a healing detoxification. Knowing the stories and learning from them helps to avoid taking in the toxin during workplace assaults in the future. We do not have to assume the role of passive victim who is paralyzed with fear and rage by toxic workplace events, behavior, and leaders. We can make apparent and transparent the harm in the story and hold it up for inspection, understanding, and sense making. Telling a story about a harmful work experience is in its essence liberating and helps to promote resilience. We can most successfully learn from experience by telling, hearing, and knowing stories from the workplace.

Potential and Reflective Space

Storytelling takes place in what Donald Winnicott (1965) called "potential space," that is, creative space, reflective space, and genuine thinking space. In a sense storytelling creates new space filled with possibilities. Telling and receiving stories constitutes a dance of sorts. For the person receiving the story, it involves not only hearing but listening deeply (Stein, 1994) to the account of the experience the other person is sharing. Such listening involves being emotionally present, being wholly attentive, and acknowledging the risk the person is taking in telling the story. The listener's attentiveness is not only to the words and stories but also to the emotions conveyed, revealing the whole person of the storyteller. And as part of the storytelling listeners have to be aware of the effect of the story on them, as revealed in their own unconscious (called reveries in psychoanalysis). This amounts to a double, or deep, listening. Both listening to the other person and attending to the emotional effect the other person has on the listener are important (Stein, 1994). The potential space of storytelling is, then, a place of great interpersonal intimacy arising from mutual trust and respect. Deep listening includes deep knowing, bearing witness, validation, and compassion. We discuss this aspect of storytelling and listening to a greater extent in the closing chapters.

Persecutory Versus Potential Space

Deep listening transforms the persecutory nature of workplace stories into potential space. Potential space offers the possibility of release—of both storyteller and listener—rather than continued imprisonment within the story and the workplace experience, which may well live on as an endless mental loop. Potential space also creates a form of inoculation against future exposure to persecutory workplace experience. Multiple exposures to being in the workplace and retelling our stories allow us to practice keeping what began outside ourselves at work from becoming part of our inner self. Storytelling provides detoxification and immunization from the harm through a two-step process. First, we can use storytelling to externalize the experience. Second, storytelling has put the experience out there for all to hear as well as hold and bear witness to, and storytelling prevents what is outside from getting back inside. For instance, what is happening in the moment at work may seem familiar, even uncanny. The same scenario is recurring, and now I know how it ends. This reflective appreciation sets in motion the possibility of acting to void revictimization.

If a storyteller begins by saying of workplace assaults, "This is what repeatedly happened to me," the storyteller becomes able to say, "This doesn't have to happen to me." Further, whereas the employee originally thinks himself to be the problem—after all, that is what others accused him of—he becomes able to say, "I am not the problem; this other person is the problem." The storyteller shifts from blaming herself and accusing herself of making all this up to being able to affirm that this really happened. Certainly the victim may consciously and unconsciously play a role in creating this externally imposed harm. Further, people must acknowledge that their own behavior may, for conscious and unconscious reasons, provoke harm by others. Someone like this can retreat to the unquestioned familiar, creating a ritual of abuse and suffering. We in no way discount this dynamic. However, we also do not wish to blame the victim for being abused, even if the victim remains in an abusive relationship with familiar dynamics.

The process by which stories detoxify and avoid further toxification amounts to an intersubjective dance of "sense making." Being validated by another person—the listener to the story—makes the teller able to validate herself. Put differently, the storyteller first experiences herself as a passive object to which the terrible things happen, creating in turn a persecutory internal world. Through internalization the assailant comes to occupy the storyteller's own inner space, in part through the defense of identifying with the aggressor. The victim then punishes and persecutes herself in the absence of the tormentor.

Through the detoxification process we are describing, the storyteller develops the beginning of more benevolent internal objects—supportive, soothing internal objects—and the capacity to distance herself from events so she can more objectively observe what happened. As a result a new frame of reference emerges. Through the experience of being emotionally contained and held by the listener, the storyteller no longer feels compelled to serve as a container for others' violent outbursts. The storyteller comes to affirm herself and say confidently, "You couldn't make this stuff up."

How does anyone understand organizational dynamics of this nature amid or at least cognizant of the massive corporate failures and bankruptcies from recent years? The balance of the book offers a humble attempt to provide insights into this question. We begin the next chapter with a discussion of some key psychoanalytic concepts that will serve as signposts in the stories that follow.

CHAPTER 3

Psychoanalytic Perspectives and the Workplace

To understand why a leader, manager, employee, or a group of executives or employees think, feel, and act the way they do requires an understanding of individual and group dynamics. These dynamics are often driven by unconscious and irrational factors that are out of awareness and not accessible to analysis using quantitative methods or theories not grounded in psychoanalytically informed perspectives. Why he, she, or they did what they did always contains hard-to-locate and -understand unconscious dynamics that are most often ignored because they are too messy and time consuming to pay attention to, not readily managed, if at all. What is going on under the surface can be exceptionally stable and unaffected by others and events or ever changing in order to cope with the distressing experience of anxiety, making meaningful change in either case an exceptional challenge. We will use here some of the well-accepted perspectives of psychoanalysis and therapy, but we have adapted them to the workplace. They are, we argue here, a way of understanding hard-to-believe leader, group, and organizational dynamics.

We also want to note that while these ideas use words like *splitting, projection,* and *transference,* they are readily understood and can be located in everyday experience at work and in life outside work. They are also grounded in a long process of theory building that spans more than a century. They are not new and have been subjected to scrutiny and revision by practitioners and scholars.

33

In this chapter we provide definitions and examples of the key psychoanalytic perspectives that we use in the rest of the book to explore the subtext of workplace stories. We ground the theory in practice and the practice in theory, hoping to make the stories more accessible and usable for readers. We will describe and define the terms in plain English and provide concrete examples so that readers may understand how the terms are applied in practice. We could but will not provide long lists of references of distinguished authors on these subjects, preferring instead to focus simply on explaining and applying these psychoanalytic perspectives to the workplace. However, we wish to acknowledge the contributions of Melanie Klein, Thomas Ogden, Donald Winnicott, and Wilfred Bion.

Overview

Throughout this book we rely on theory primarily grounded in object relations theorizing, which not only embraces unconscious individual processes but also focuses on the interpersonal world. The fundamental terms of object relations ideas that we use here are *splitting, projection,* and *projective identification.* These are often accompanied by *transference* and *countertransference,* which involve unconsciously transferring or relocating in the present an experience from the past, along with its accompanying thoughts, feelings, and actions, as well as consistently relied-upon psychological defenses. Together these five concepts explain unconscious intrapersonal and interpersonal dynamics that can be extended to group processes. To these concepts we add two concepts from interpersonal and group dynamics—the role of *containment* in the workplace and *holding environments.*

To begin we need to differentiate *our* use of unconscious process from the use of unconscious in a *clinical* sense. People always think, feel, and do things that may be described as underpinned by unconscious process. These unconscious processes may be described using the terms we have just introduced and will discuss in this chapter. However, these processes also imply deeper unconscious dynamics unique to each of us. Overreaction to a powerful authority figure may occur unless someone can point out to us that the sources of our reactions are the relationships we had with a parent, sibling, or other relative early in life. In a sense, without this appreciation we are simply left to accept that this is how we are. Based on distressing prior life experience, we may overreact to being touched, ordered around, manipulated, or not rewarded for our work.

In sum, we differentiate between specific unconscious processes like splitting and projection and the unconscious that lies beneath psychologically defensive processes. Our focus is on the manifestations of a deeper unconscious dynamic that metaphorically provides a window for therapists to view the disturbed qualities of the patient. It is a way of peering into the soul. By being aware of and observing (through their own emotional response) such processes as splitting, projection, and transference, as well as other psychologically defensive dynamics, therapists have a view of the underlying psychodynamics that result in these thoughts, feelings, and behaviors. In saying this we wish to make clear we are not attempting to psychoanalyze the people in our stories (or at work) in terms of this deeper and clinical aspect of our unconscious selves. Rather we focus on how the presence of unconscious processes like splitting, projection, and transference affect our lives at work. We believe that in this appreciation lies more self-awareness and insight, as well as improved awareness and insight into the actions of others and the group dynamics that share many of these unconscious processes.

Splitting and Projection

Splitting is an unconscious thought process most often described as a response to a distressing experience (a defensive response) in which one divides oneself or the image of another individual or group so that one side of the split is good and the other is bad. Splitting is facilitated by denial of the split-off self and associated experience. For example, someone may deny he is enraged and locate the anger in another person, whose calm attributes he denies. Denial as a psychological defense removes the distressing content from immediate awareness. The sequence is first that the person denies the distressing experience and then splits it off. Splitting also occurs as part of a process that includes projection and projective identification, which we will discuss later. It is essential to speak of splitting and projection as occurring together, even though they may be discussed separately. In the first example, of the enraged person, it is not entirely possible or meaningful to discuss splitting in the workplace without allowing for projection.

We emphasize that splitting is a mental process but one that can be shared by others who find themselves in the same or similarly distressing experience, thereby creating a sense of a bond. For instance, a person may feel attacked, victimized, abused, bullied, unacknowledged, put down, and ignored by another individual, who is perhaps a supervisor or manager and whom the victim comes to see as not good, bad, and even evil. Many people may arrive at this splitting independently or together with others. This process in fact happens so often that it fades into the background, out of awareness. In a sense the world becomes black and white with no middle ground. We should also acknowledge here the other side of the equation, so to speak. To the extent that employees have compelling and overdetermined needs (that is, needs arising from unconscious psychological factors) to be rewarded, liked, and admired, it is more likely the supervisor or manager will not measure up and will be identified as bad as a result of inadvertently creating harm by not appreciating the compelling nature of these needs. At a group level the finance department and its desire to manage costs may conflict with the marketing department, which needs a bigger budget and an organizational willingness to accept more risk to make more sales. At a global level the language of splitting is evident when leaders point out evil doers, an axis of evil, and evil empires, labels that speak to international cultural and religion-based clashes. In all these cases leaders direct attention to the external threat, leading almost magically to greater group cohesion to defend against the threat while also ignoring that the leader(s) might be ineffective and perhaps harm the group and its members by taking their resources for personal benefit.

Paradoxically splitting may also occur in the reverse. People may see themselves as weak, ineffective, unworthy of respect and admiration, and in general bad. Through idealization they then see the other person or group as good and possessing many admirable qualities, such as leading and acting effectively, being worthy of admiration and respect, and perhaps exhibiting a willingness to look out for everyone else. When a new manager, executive, or CEO shows up in a workspace, others may immediately feel less important, less effective, and less empowered, even fearful of this powerful leader. In the employees' minds this individual becomes bigger than life, while they feel diminished in the leader's presence.

Splitting combined with projection, we want to note, occurs in everyone and with enough frequency to affect how we experience ourselves and others. The splits may also be durable and stable once they arise, and, because they largely exist out of awareness, they are not particularly open to self-inspection. This narrowed self-awareness and awareness of others simply is the way things are and is not open to questioning, perhaps until a critical event calls the leader into question. Only then do people notice that the leader is human after all. It is also often the case that if a colleague points out the existence of these splits, the employees may well defend the splits and ignore the colleague's comments rather than explore them in terms of their meaning.

Last, we wish to emphasize that while splitting is common and natural, it also degrades accurate reality testing. People create in their minds a context that is not exactly accurate or true. It is, however, comforting in terms of coping with distressing anxiety. And at an extreme, splitting can promote thinking, feeling, and actions that are destructive in the sense that the other person, group, or nation becomes regarded as despicable and evil vermin, making its destruction by any means seem perfectly reasonable. This dynamic is what creates the hostile takeovers, dominance, submission, and such massive cultural dislocations as the genocides all too common in the twentieth and twenty-first centuries.

An Example of Splitting

In this example we focus on splitting, but because, as we mentioned, it cannot be entirely understood without also considering projection, the example includes projection.

Tom is an engineer and owner of a company with nearly five hundred employees. Upon being hired into an upper-management position, Jim finds that Tom is not only admired but almost adored by many managers and employees. He almost walks on water. He had founded the company to manufacture and market unique environmental monitoring equipment, and no company has yet created competing versions. His company is in a safe niche. Employees feel secure and the pay is good. The company is growing. This is what attracted Jim to the company.

Jim feels strongly encouraged by his colleagues to join in their mutual admiration society that places Tom on a pedestal. Almost all employees feel that he is superior to them in most ways, and Tom seems to appreciate this, basking in the warm glow of employee approval. Jim, however, has worked at several other companies with similar dynamics and is not eager to join in this shared idealization. These former employers of Jim's ultimately went bankrupt because the leaders had mismanaged the companies. Jim has become a skeptic and needs to see that, based on Tom's actions, the admiration is merited. Jim is, in effect, not willing to deny and split off his experience of himself as competent and capable or deny and split off aspects of Tom that do not support the idealization of him. Jim nonetheless feels a real sense of social pressure to do so. Jim's unwillingness to join in what amounts to a somewhat delusional conspiracy has attracted the attention of his colleagues.

Jim learns within his first few months of employment that some employees have left the company. He hears stories about people who questioned or crossed Tom and who were abruptly fired. In the background Tom is feared, which paradoxically enhances the high regard in which he is held. Gradually Jim, in observing Tom, sees him as surrounded by adoring sycophants, and Jim sees some of the same underlying management trends that occurred in the two companies he worked for that went bankrupt. He also understands that calling into question these dynamics based on splitting is not going to promote his career development in the company. In a way, by not joining in the splitting, he becomes a participant-observer who is doing his job and not infrequently checking out job sites on the Internet. He, too, might end up suddenly fired as not fitting in or lose his job because the company is failing.

Projection is a companion dynamic to denial and splitting. Projection gets rid of distressing self-experience relative to another by locating it elsewhere in one's mind. The other person becomes a representation and embodiment created and then manipulated in one's mind. To put it colloquially, the content projected is not experienced inside oneself but out there as an attribute of you, the Other. We always know others and groups in part in this way—a self-creation. Once again this is so common and so natural as to most often happen without awareness, and therefore it is unappreciated and not open to reflection. It is common to hear different views of one individual from a number of people, all of whom have come to know him in different ways—some good and some bad.

Underlying projection is a hard-to-resolve conflict of trying to imagine oneself or another person as having both good and bad qualities at the same time. Liking and hating someone at the same time is a tough challenge. When this conflict becomes difficult to manage, the split, and its projection onto the internal representation of the other person, simplifies life. It is simply easier to experience oneself as the victim, or good, and the other person as the victimizer, or bad. Once the projection takes place, there is an unconscious investment in maintaining the projection, leading to denial of conflicting information. Since everyone has both good and bad aspects, this outcome bends reality to one's own needs.

We also need to point out that while projection takes place in one's mind, the results of the splitting and projection do tend to leak out into the interpersonal world and between groups. The result of splitting and projection inadvertently leads to acting in ways relative to the other person that are consistent with the split but disconnected to some extent from the actual other person. In turn this person may have some sense of being seen in a certain way that does not fit with her own self-conception. The individual receiving the projections may not feel that she is especially bad and continually victimizing the other person. This is a common aspect of interpersonal and intergroup relations that often remains at the margins of awareness and is most often not open to reflection, inspection, and discussion—and therefore to change. Challenging the leaking projections may in fact serve only as a proof of sorts that the person is indeed bad and in denial.

An Example of Projection

In the first example Tom in nearly everyone's mind is superior, if not almost godlike. They see him as an idealized leader possessing all the knowledge, information, and answers to lead the company forward. As a result many members of the organization feel they are inferior to Tom and have assumed a role of dependence on him in the hope he will take care of them, their careers, their personal development, and their salaries. When others discuss Tom, they do so as if he is nearly perfect, all powerful, and even omniscient. Whenever Jim probes or calls into question these images of Tom, others defend their conception of him and have shown a willingness to see Jim as bad for raising questions. This results in occasional personal attacks on Jim as not being a team player. Further, those who regard Tom as nearly perfect often act as though this is true, as is the way of sycophants and others who idealize a leader. Tom is of course influenced by this and comes to feel more important as a result of the constant pressure of leaked splitting and projections that influence the actions, thoughts, and feelings of his employees toward him. Others often wait for Tom to make all the decisions, in a sense inducing him to do so by their waiting. This is a subtle but also powerful process that, while observable, is also usually unacknowledged and undiscussable. To speak of it would threaten the individual and shared splitting and projection. "This is how we do things here" is a common phrase that warns, "Do not question it."

Projective Identification

In projective identification a person not only acts as though the other person is the embodiment of the internal image but also actively encourages the other person or group to act in accordance with that image. The process is more forceful than the example of simply waiting for Tom to make all the decisions. In fact projective identification is forceful enough that some analysts consider it a form of interpersonal aggression and even violence, an effort to try to take over the other person. In clinical practice it can also be understood as a form of communication. Much the same can be said to occur between groups, divisions in organizations, and even between countries on a global scale. The fundamental nature of projective identification is not only to impose the projections on an external person—sometimes called an object—but also to have the other person accept or take in the projections, thereby becoming more like the projections. This acceptance of the projections distinguishes projective identification from projection. The other person becomes, at least in the moment, changed by the process. This dynamic largely takes place out of awareness. The other person or group becomes more like what is implicitly desired in the projections in order to reduce anxiety or other distressing experience on both sides of the process. The other individual or group can be known in a way consistent with a split-off and projected mental image. All is well, then, for the person engaged in splitting and projection. And for the recipient the constant pressure to become like the projected content diminishes, thereby relieving anxiety. When achieved, projective identification clearly alters reality testing in both the projector and target. This projective knowing of the self-created object is part of a psychologically defensive and unconscious process that began in one person's mind, largely independent of reality.

We emphasize once again that this is all quite natural and usually occurs outside of awareness. It is simply how humans operate. What is important to appreciate is that these dynamics are going on all the time among most of those around us. Think for a moment of young teens in love. The boy sees the girl as beautiful and desirable, fulfilling his fantasies and desires. She is perfect or nearly so. Accordingly he then not only acts as though she is perfect, he also wants her to feel this way and continually nurtures this self-experience in her. With time she becomes in her mind the beautiful and desired object, radiating a sense of everything desired by her boyfriend. She has in a sense become what the boy desires. Conversely her inner image of the boy steers him gradually to fulfill her construction of him in her mind. If she desires a powerful and bold male who is also sensitive to her needs, she will constantly be coaching him to fulfill her vision of him. He is rewarded for his desirable behavior and may be punished for his less desirable behavior. All is well between them as each is gradually shaped by the other to fulfill an idealized and anxiety-reducing counterpart based on splitting and projection. In a sense each becomes lost in the other as unconscious contracting, collusion, and mutual adjustment occurs. In the process both have at least temporarily lost parts of themselves that are not consistent with the projections, and they have assumed parts and roles that are new and different and perhaps not really who they are. Dynamics like this also take place at work, especially between leaders and followers.

An Example of Projective Identification

In the story Tom is idealized by many of his staff and employees. He is bigger than life and is thought to be able to lead with near perfection. Why not? He has so far created a company, grown it in size, and at the same time made some employees who joined him early on very wealthy while paying everyone else well. This process of idealization is in large part based on projective identification: Tom has become like the image that many employees have come to share about how Tom should be. This reduces their distress and anxiety and makes them feel good.

Those who do not join in this dynamic are ignored or even eliminated from the organization. The employees do more than simply wait expectantly for Tom to make all the decisions. They actively encourage him to feel a sense of greatness and infallibility, which feeds his ego. He is continually complimented and stroked by his staff and employees. He has in a sense been slowly and carefully coached into being the leader they desire. He has all the responsibility. He makes all the decisions. He shelters his employees from distressing problems with operations and competitors. He is expected to take care of everyone, much as a loving father does his children. Tom eventually accepts this constant press of projections onto him, and he comes to experience himself as a truly superior human being with outstanding management and leadership skills. He now has an expansive sense of his abilities, feeling he is infallible and must therefore make all the decisions.

A dynamic like this often occurs in organizations. This in turn promotes projections by others onto the executives, creating a mutual admiration echo chamber that can lead to feelings of ever-greater omnipotence. The world is in good order for everyone, right up to the point that reality bursts this bubble, as in the case of bankruptcy.

The counterpart of the development of a projective identification like this is that Tom, by accepting the idealizing projections, correspondingly has to eliminate self-experience that is not consistent with the idealization. In his mind he splits off his imperfections and limitations and projects them onto his marginally capable and even childlike employees, whom he must then command, control, and take care of, which also fulfills their vision of him. He encourages them to feel as though they are not capable and competent, and they in turn accept this view of themselves and become like Tom's projections, as he evacuates his own imperfections and limitations and locates them in those around him. This dynamic has a balance that creates the echo chamber. The employees now feel less than capable and need to be taken care of by their now grandiose leader, who steps forward to do so. In a sense this is a transaction in which all the competence rests with Tom and the incompetence with the employees.

Jim, if he is not careful, will be pegged as a naysayer, not a team player, and someone disconnected from the shared fantasy of the greatness of Tom as a leader. Jim may persist in his position by saying little, essentially taking cover in a metaphoric organizational foxhole. However, this might also not be possible since not being an active supporter of this projection-based dynamic is still seen as a threat to others, who at some level are easily threatened by anyone who does not support their splitting and projection. Accurate reality testing is to be avoided.

Transference

The workplace is filled with feelings not related to performing one's work or that of the organization. Transference is most fundamentally the transfer of feelings from the past to the present, and this transfer distorts thoughts, feelings, and actions in the present. A supervisor who looks like, sounds like, or acts like a parent (or previous supervisor or authority figure) who was abusive, manipulative, or unavailable for nurturing will frequently evoke feelings consistent with how an employee experienced the parental figure. The supervisor's behavior may unwittingly evoke transference if it resembles the past experience of the parental figure, with the result that the feelings evoked in the moment are overly strong and not consistent with the supervisor's actual behavior. The response is disproportionate and might be referred to as a hot button. The individual may become overly fearful, submissive, adoring, enraged, or withdrawn and retreat from contact.

This response is deeply ingrained and is a system of defensive responses to the relationship between the child and parental figure or other significant figure as an adult. It works most of the time to relieve distress and anxiety. The supervisor may be aware that the employee's response is not consistent with what the supervisor said or did but at the same time is taken aback by the response, wondering what she did to receive this response. This suggests that it would be useful to consider the role of transference in terms of projective identification, where this overdetermined response may be viewed as training the supervisor to respond in a different way, for example by becoming the parental figure the employee always wanted.

Transference may thus be understood to blur reality, where, in conjunction with splitting and projection, it may well further aggravate the connection with, as in the last example, an ominous or idealized supervisor. The supervisor is created in the employee's mind through splitting and projection, perhaps in a manner consistent with how the employees manipulated in their minds authority figures or parental figures in the past. The splitting and projection are deeply ingrained unconscious defenses the child learned by trial and error while trying to find a way to cope with the parental figure's abuse, dominance, engulfment, abandonment, emotional unavailability, and unpredictable behavior—to list but some of the more devastating losses of adequate caretaking. The same can be said for previous experience with supervisors, managers, and organizations. The outcome of this relatively stable defensive pattern of splitting and projection is that it informs the understanding of transference relative to an individual constructed at first in someone's mind and then as an external object who is encouraged to accept the projections (projective identification), becoming what the employee desires in order to reduce distress and anxiety.

An Example of Transference

Tom is a grand, heroic, almost omniscient leader who created the company and has thus far led it to success, benefiting all the employees who admire and idealize him in ways that are not always consistent with reality—of which Jim tends to remind others. Tom has in part been created by the employees and, having accepted many of their projections, has become more like what they want, evoking feelings consistent with those toward a desirable authority figure from the past lives of the employees, who in turn gradually come to share many of the same positive feelings. The transfer of past feelings to Tom in the present is consistent with their feelings about similar figures from their previous life experiences (or in fantasy) who were powerful and who provided good nurturing and caretaking. All those who have largely unconsciously joined together in a form of collusive behavior to create an idealized vision of Tom also then feel good about him. These feelings, while different for each employee, are also similar in their overall nature. Most people share a common conception of and wish for a nurturing and caretaking symbolic parent. Similarly Tom's transference may well be in a manner consistent with parenting and caring for children.

In sum, the emotions associated with attachment to the parental figure are simply transferred to Tom, toward whom the feelings include a sense of merger, bonding, secure attachment, caretaking, security, and even love. People feel safe in their role as employees and in turn become uncritically joined with Tom, who is their wise and caretaking parental figure. Last, it is important to note that a similar dynamic can create a leader who is bad or evil and employees who are good and being victimized. We underscore this appreciation in the stories that follow.

Containment

Containment, as we are using the term, was first described by Wilfred Bion (1961, 1962). Containment in a clinical sense refers to an infant, child, or adult who, through projective identification, locates distressing self-experience and awareness in another individual who possesses sufficient personal integrity to receive and retain this uncanny content without becoming too anxious and retaliate. This in turn allows for the content to eventually be taken back (reintegrated). We have adapted this concept to the workplace. In particular we view an effective leader as one who serves as a temporary container for all manner of projections but also disruptive thoughts, feelings, and behavior such as confusion, fear, and anger. This leader is able to absorb these often emotion-filled and psychologically defensive dynamics without losing self-integration.

By doing so the leader allows others to feel calmer and under control, either as a result of the leader's temporarily accepting the projections and efforts at projective identification or by accepting and acknowledging that others may feel confused, fearful, or angry. By sensing this cognitive and affective experience (not shutting it out or defending against it), the leader must, in order to contain it, not become personally disorganized, anxious, and psychologically defensive. A response like this is experienced by many as calming and soothing and not unlike that of a parental figure who calms and soothes the small child; the leader becomes the focal point of positive transference arising from caretaking parental figures. Moreover, if necessary, the leader sets boundaries on behavior if it becomes interpersonally or organizationally destructive, further containing these dynamics. While some people may resent being stopped, others appreciate the willingness to stop the behavior to maintain some sense of order and civility. We note that anyone who is able to do this important work is serving as a leader, regardless of title.

In sum, a leader who fulfills a role of containment is nondefensively immersed in the distress, anxiety-ridden, and psychologically defensive experience of employees and at the same time is able to maintain sufficient interpersonal distance to be minimally affected. The result is that, while the leader is being watched by many for her reaction, she creates a calm affect and context that permits reflective practice on the part of almost everyone. We acknowledge that this treatment of containment may differ from the work of some authors and clinical theory. Adapting this theory to the workplace is a creative act.

An Example of Containment

While Tom is a leader with big and successful ideas, from Jim's perspective Tom does not pay enough attention to the details of administration and fiscal affairs, including how his ideas are implemented. This dynamic continually creates crises that cause his employees to look to Tom to straighten everything out. Tom, Jim realizes, almost enjoys these challenges. Tom is calm, cool, and collected and invariably makes his employees feel that they can overcome the operating problems that he paradoxically has a role in creating. His presence draws people together with a can-do feeling. His ability to be calm in a storm of problems and to draw people together to solve them is highly admired, contributing to his idealization. He seems fully engaged and aware and able to think critically during these crises.

However, from Jim's perspective, Tom is not actually all that effective at figuring out what to do; sometimes he creates more problems. Further, many people ignore that the root cause of the problems is Tom's inattention to the details of running the company. Also implicit in Tom's response is a process of infantilizing the employees: he, as the father figure, must take care of his childlike employees, who, as Tom sees it, have created the problem. Thus Tom's leadership has pluses and minuses, and the darker side does not receive attention. This is sometimes referred to as selective attention and, more darkly, as denial and rationalization.

Holding Environment

We suggest that it is worthwhile to consider the notion of a holding environment in conjunction with the idea of workplace containment. This notion, formulated by Donald Winnicott, began as a clinical perspective that explores the relationship between mother and infant. Most fundamentally *holding* refers to the calming, soothing, and safety of an infant being held by its mother. Beyond this is the ability of the mother to imagine the infant's experience and needs in order to envelop the infant in a caretaking context that anticipates the infant's needs. This is a profoundly intimate and personal experience that also speaks to these same needs later in life at work. In the workplace a leader or leaders can metaphorically hold the organization and the experience of its members, thereby creating calming, soothing, and safe individual and shared experience. When a crisis occurs, how often do groups look for someone to lead them from their desert of despair? And conversely, when all is well, the role of the leader, or at least his presence, is less essential and ignored or even disparaged as controlling, limiting, and judgmental as a result of holding people accountable. The leader in this context is metaphorically left to smash the tablets on the ground.

Thus a close connection exists between a leader containing distressing experience and anxiety and providing a safe-enough holding environment. We suggest that each, while qualitatively different, depends on and interacts with the other. During good times stresses are manageable, as is workplace anxiety, minimizing the need for psychologically defensive dynamics but also in a sense minimizing the latent containing and holding potential of the leader. In contrast, when things are falling apart and everyone is anxious, psychologically defensive dynamics emerge. This latent potential then emerges and is appreciated, assuming that the leader is capable of containing and holding and does not personally become disorganized and ineffective or actually contribute to the dynamic.

An Example of Holding

Tom is pretty calm when it comes to crises and able to calm the employees and engage them in problem solving, which he often also directs. Most of the time he is also disengaged from most aspects of running the company, preferring to focus on developing new ideas in his office and networking with other CEOs around the country. When problems do occur, he is most often there as a calming but also caretaking presence. He not only helps his employees engage in problem solving; he also makes them feel safe, secure, and taken care of. He is there metaphorically to bandage their knee if they fall and to give them a hug before sending them out to solve the problem. At times Tom brings a sense of playfulness to the work. The challenge of solving problems is stimulating, and he makes sure successes are celebrated. Tom is most often warm and affectionate, and everyone feels a little bit loved. Jim is respectful of Tom's fulfilling this important role and most often senses a real authenticity to what Tom feels and thinks and does for his employees. Tom seems to really care.

Conclusion

We acknowledge that we have adapted the use of these terms and the well-accepted theory that lies behind them to the workplace and in this process constructively modified them. Even so, the theory provides important insights into how to understand workplace experience, including managing and consulting with it. It is important to consider this perspective when trying to understand the workplace. This is underscored by the stories in part 2 that explore the darker side of our organizations. We have selected the ideas used here for their unusual ability to peel back interpersonal and organizational dynamics for inspection.

We also acknowledge that other viable psychodynamically and psychosocially informed perspectives are available to explore the subjective and intersubjective nature of the workplace. In fact we do insert other perspectives in our discussion of the stories where appropriate. We do not attempt here to magically fit the stories into a single integrated perspective. Life at work is messier than that.

As you read, we encourage you to pause at the list of questions after each story. What questions come to mind in addition to these? Taking this moment to reflect will contribute to your exploring our discussion of the stories. What did we miss? How does the story relate to your own experience or that of others? And if it does relate, what questions do you ask of this experience for yourself?

PART TWO

STORIES AND ANALYSIS

This book is fundamentally but not exclusively about stories that illuminate the dark side of the workplace. Some stories tell of successes in turning around the dark side to create an enjoyable and productive place to work. The stories we provide are drawn from our experiences. Some stories are also based on stories told to us and stories drawn from our observations of events in our workplaces and in our consulting work. These stories really did happen. We have modified them to avoid identifying the specific organizations and people involved.

The stories are paired with lists of questions to encourage you, the reader, to take a moment to reflect on the story as well as on your experiences at work. We conclude each story with our own analysis, which is informed by the psychoanalytic theory we discussed in chapter 3. We occasionally add other insights that help in understanding the complexity of the story. We once again invite you, the reader, to reflect on our analysis. Did we think of everything? Most certainly we have not thought of everything. Further, the similar experiences you have had provide opportunities to better understand not only the story as told but your own stories as well. Last, the stories as groups highlight the vast array of experience one can have at work that has its origin in human nature and one's unconscious underpinnings.

CHAPTER 4

Destructive Leaders and Organizational Darkness

Introduction

Leaders ranging from presidents and CEOs all the way down to local supervisors and leaders of temporary teams can and do have a powerful influence on individual and group experience. Words like *toxic, toxicity,* and *pathological* are fairly common adjectives applied to leaders, who are sometimes portrayed in movies and TV series as antiheroes. We humbly wish to add the following stories ripped from the pages of actual life experience. Our experience, as employees, executives, academics, and consultants, has been that leaders can and often do have a powerfully negative influence on organizational life and organizational functioning.

We readily acknowledge that positive stories are not covered in equal numbers in this book, but we include some in which the darkness is lifted by leaders who are effective at working with people and at fulfilling their management responsibilities. We, however, remain struck—if not stupefied—by how disruptive, destructive, and dysfunctional leaders in powerful roles can be. And we suggest that when people encounter them, these leaders are always remembered as the figurative hot stove to be avoided at all costs, even though quitting is not often a good option. Also, the corporate culture of the employee's next job may be no healthier, perhaps as a result of the nature and ubiquity of these destructive leaders. Deeply embedded personality structures enable them to obtain leadership roles, which they may also diligently seek out.

Each of the dozen stories that follow illustrates aspects of work life that people may encounter during their career. Each story provides a different insight into what seems to be all-too-familiar leadership and organizational dysfunction. These stories also illustrate that things all too often are not logical or rational at work, and sometimes illogical decisions are made for illogical reasons. We will let the stories tell the tale of the dysfunctional workplace. We provide thought-provoking questions after each story, and we provide our insights into the stories using a psychodynamically informed perspective enhanced, where appropriate, by other perspectives.

STORY I
FAILURE IS AN OPTION

Samuel, a consultant, was contacted by the new CEO of a division of a corporation that marketed a variety of products. The CEO asked him: "Could you arrive in a day or two at the site of a telephone marketing group?" That the request carried a grave sense of urgency was clear.

Upon arriving Samuel was given a quick orientation by on-site management. It included an account of what had led up to the near-catastrophic current problems. The president of the corporation had purchased the marketing organization two years earlier and learned the software it was using was out of date and had serious issues. A nationally prominent consulting company had been contracted to bring in state-of-the-art software eighteen months before. The consulting company proceeded to use new software packages from several of its corporate partners.

The consulting company proposed use of a database product that on-site management did not think would work, but the president, located five hundred miles away, nonetheless decided to adopt it. To the database product was added another one for managing shipping and inventory and a third product for billing. Further, the system had to be adapted to a preexisting corporate accounting system. In order to do this, programmers had to build bridges so the noncompatible software packages could interface. Moreover, the president rejected the consulting company's proposal to create management reports, preferring instead to save money by using his own IT staff to do this important work at some time in the future. The bridge building was still underway after eighteen months and the investment of millions of dollars.

While this work was proceeding, the president announced to stockholders that he would have the new system up and running on July 1. As

July approached, the consulting company had not finished its work and told the president that it needed many more months to do so. Despite this information, the president ordered that the new software would go live on July 1. He also turned off the old billing system, even though running parallel systems would have provided the opportunity to retreat to the old system if the new system did not work out. From the start none of the systems worked—order taking, shipping, billing, and accounting. The client company fired and then sued the consulting company. After the marketing organization had been struggling for twelve weeks, the division CEO had called Samuel.

The lack of functioning interfaces caused the bridging software to reject all new orders. Orders were placed in edit files, which now contained more than two months of orders, most of which had not shipped. (Rejected orders are placed in computer generated files based on the type of error and are therefore referred to as edit files.)

These problems were aggravated by the sales staff, which was entering orders in a system that was not user friendly and had parts that did not work. The staff had come up with ways to work around these problems to take orders from customers over the phone, but this required leaving data elements, such as credit card numbers and the ship-by date, blank.

Staff members, who had limited IT experience and no training on the new system, were slowly figuring out where all the shipping edit files were in the system, a process that continued for months. The lack of any management reporting further compounded the problems. (Management reporting consists of reports management receives about the number and dollar value of sales, how orders were placed, who took the orders, shipping dates, etc.) Once the edit files were found, they contained thousands of orders, and each order had to be manually manipulated in order to get it shipped, which was the top priority—customer service. A team of employees eventually worked on this full time. The shipping system was able to ship products but had not been set up to handle inventory management. As a result stock was counted manually and reordered.

More specifically, during the first three months most orders taken could not be shipped due to missing or incomplete data elements. The software bridge—software that permits two different software packages to communicate—to the shipping software rejected the orders, placing them into edit files dependent on the type of missing or incomplete data. These files had to be worked manually and individually, and it was common that one rejection would be resolved only to have other orders also be rejected and placed in new shipping edit files, resulting in the product order not being shipped. Once an order was successfully shipped the bridge to the billing software rejected many of the shipped orders for billing. This led to yet another round of manual interventions to get the shipped order billed. And even if the billing went out and was paid, applying the payments to accounts in the corporate accounting system were rejected by yet another bridge requiring even more manual interventions.

Paradoxically, staff members had good morale despite being vastly impaired in their work. They had a sense of rising to the occasion and "taking the beach" despite enemy fire. They were having some success in mastering a nearly impossible challenge. They described the president, former consulting company, and home office, and the layer of marginally competent backbiting sycophants that staffed it, as laughable cartoon figures that could not walk and chew gum.

Samuel facilitated this work, provided interim leadership during crisis management (a daily event), and helped the local leaders find ways they could work more effectively to support their staff. After the work on the edit lists was going reasonably well, he began to focus on the underlying problems that had generated the vast mess. Inevitably this implicated those loyal to the president in the home office who had played a role in creating the disaster. Samuel uncovered one problem after another in group sessions with the staff. However, within these task groups were loyalists to the home office, people who reported the problems being found to their contacts there. Others regarded these loyalists as receiving special status and viewed them with suspicion. The snake pit soon managed to get Samuel taken out. His unearthing of an endless number of poor design and management decisions did not make those bonded to the president look good.

The organization never overcame all these self-generated obstacles. The new division CEO, who had hired Samuel originally, worked to improve sales during the next six months in anticipation of selling the company as soon as possible. He lost his position at about the time of the sale and was made the scapegoat for the failure by the president, who explained to stockholders what had happened.

Questions

How does this story challenge the assumption that technical or technological solutions stand apart from psychological considerations, that psychodynamics do not influence or contaminate IT decisions?

What were the president's conscious and unconscious priorities?

In what ways does the unfolding of the story illustrate the vicious downward spiral of organizational self-destruction?

Why did the president insist on "going live on July 1" with the new computer software?

What were some of the consequences for the corporation of the president's leadership style and decision making?

How did the staff compensate for the president's irrational, erratic, and unrealistic behavior?

Discussion and Analysis

The notion that presidents, CEOs, and managers are rational decision makers who maximize performance and wealth is far more often a fantasy than a reality. Sometimes making decisions that will create catastrophic failure is a viable option if the unspoken goal is to protect oneself against looking ineffective and not in control to stockholders and stock analysts. In our story releasing the software on the date announced was more important to the president than corporate survival. At least in part, narcissism and the fear of shame drive this type of psychologically defensive system. Upholding a good public appearance is paramount. Short-run illusion trumps long-term reality. Failure is regrettably often an option when narcissism and pure self-interest are of paramount importance.

In this case the president had made a public announcement to go live on July 1 and stuck to this date to avoid *looking* ineffective to stockholders. He said it would happen, and nothing could stand in the way of making it happen. The president was enabled by a layer of loyal but marginally competent senior executives who had been with him a long time. He had made them all wealthy. In turn this layer of managers recruited people loyal to them who would similarly protect them. A dynamic like this embeds this approach to management in every layer of the organization. To maintain their esteemed roles in the eyes of the president, the senior executives had to suppress recognition of problems that they had created.

The dynamics of an organization that operates like this have a profoundly negative effect on organizational performance. The workplace context is one of paranoia, fear, dominance and submission, punishment and unilateral self-protection. Everyone understood it was dangerous to work for the organization, especially if you wanted to speak up. Personal survival can become the subtext of daily work life. Improving organizational performance with a context like this fades to the background. Unconscious irrationality that introduces performance-impairing dysfunctions can become the known but unmentionable norm. The known becomes unknown and eventually unknowable.

Processes such as this one are also exacerbated by splitting and projection. The detested people in the distant home office (the snake pit) were often spoken of as the source of all problems. They were simply all bad despite some positives, such as managers who did work effectively to support their division. Similarly in the home office the staff and CEO of this division were often denigrated in meetings, targeted as the source of all the operating problems. This polarized context may not have created the situation, but it certainly aggravated it, leading to the sale of a division that was ultimately unsalvageable and the termination of its new CEO.

Finally, the president had purchased the marketing company without much knowledge or experience of how it ran. He, like countless others in positions of upper management in recent decades, came into the organization from the outside. He did not grow up, so to speak, in the organization, which in turn means that he did not know the organization or the industry from the bottom up. What is worse, he did not recognize that he lacked crucial information about the organization's history and operations. He not only didn't know what he didn't know, he also felt that he did not need to know it.

STORY 2

WAR IN THE WORKPLACE

A major service organization had a large number of powerful, geographically dispersed and specialized divisions that were strongly defended by their vice presidents. The divisions were dependent for their income on an in-house billing service. This service was led by a long-serving executive, Robert, who reported to the president. During his nearly twenty-year tenure, Robert had used his control of the information in the billing system—in addition to a considerable amount of financial information—to gain control and to defend himself, his staff, and his operation from a growing level of complaints from the division vice presidents and more specifically from their chief administrative officers (CAOs). The vice presidents wanted to know where all the money was that they thought they should have. They and their employees were highly productive, and more collections from their billing were merited.

During the previous decade the vice presidents had gradually replaced the CAOs with individuals who were more combative, arrogant, and aggressive so they could hold Robert accountable. This led to an equally energized defensive response from Robert and his staff. The gradual escalation of this dynamic led to open warfare between the divisions and the central office. No stone on this battlefield was left unturned, and most were being thrown. The battle lines were well established, familiar, and stable.

Eventually a new president yielded to pressure from the vice presidents and terminated Robert. A number of Robert's key staff also left, leaving the billing operation with little leadership. Robert's replacement, James, was confronted with this intraorganizational battlefield littered with interpersonal and financial destruction. His work was complicated by the loss of the senior staff to run the half-billion-dollar-a-year billing operation.

One of James's early decisions was to open the entire billing database to inspection by the combative CAOs. This removed all barriers to their learning why there appeared to be too little income. They had nothing left to attack. The fortress was dismantled in one stroke. Additionally James instructed his staff to stop retaliating against the divisional CAOs—something that was deeply ingrained in their behavior. This step removed one side of the nearly continuous process of attack and counterattack. Attacking someone who offers no defense is, after a while, unfulfilling. It takes all the excitement out of the battle.

James attended the regular monthly meeting of the division CAOs, who continued to remain combative. The CAOs, having killed off Robert and most of his staff, were now seeking data to show just how bad Robert and his managers had been. They wanted to justify their many accusations. Although they had been provided with unlimited access to the data, they did not explore the huge database on their own. Rather they asked one of the few remaining central office employees, Sally, to do their research for them. She was generally accepted as honest. The requests were endless, consuming much of her time for the next six months.

After several meetings in which Sally presented information, the CAOs were feeling frustrated. So far their requests for information had not yielded anything resembling a smoking gun. In fact the information basically proved they were wrong in their accusations. During one meeting their rage exploded, and they attacked everything in sight, including Sally. What was she hiding? When it was pointed out that they could inspect the data themselves, their response was equally angry. As Sally left the meeting with James, her only comment was "They hate us."

After six months the intensity of the postdeparture attack on Robert and his staff gradually abated. No smoking gun was ever found. However, James and Sally determined that the CAOs were asking the wrong questions in their effort to learn why they were not making more money. Major financial mismanagement existed within their divisions—charges were not captured, or, if they were, many were sometimes not submitted to the billing office. Additionally the CAOs and their staff members did not respond to questions from clients, who would not pay without answers to their questions about their bills. In this case Robert was writing off millions of dollars per year after waiting six months to a year for a response to client questions from the CAOs and their staffs.

As the open warfare decreased, the arrogance and aggression in the divisions still remained just below the surface and would pop up from time to time. Further, even though the CAOs and their key staff members received training on how to use the billing system to generate their own analyses, they did not initiate their own inquiries. As time passed it became abundantly clear that most problems regarding lost income lay within the divisions. At least one vice president fired his CAO for gross mismanagement, sending a signal to the other vice presidents and their CAOs. The president pressed other vice presidents to get their divisions in order. They in turn pressured their CAOs, who were then reenergized to attack the billing office, saying all the problems in lost income were in the billing office. After three years only modest improvements had been achieved in the divisions, despite a number of attention-getting failures on the part of the CAOs.

Questions

How often are organizational dynamics dominated by internal rivalries and conflict?

How often are organizational resources manipulated and used to get people fired by withholding the resources they need to do their jobs?

What role do injuries to excessive pride and narcissism play in creating vindictiveness and personal attacks that may have few limits in terms of vanquishing the offending person or group?

In what ways can scapegoating and blaming others protect an individual or group from being held accountable?

What are some ways that leaders can avoid, change, or stop organizational dynamics like this, such as simply ordering them to stop?

When emotions run hot at work, how likely is it that everyone can cease hostilities long enough to inspect the data and situation in order to understand it?

Discussion and Analysis

This is a story about how a deeply embedded set of behaviors becomes the way the company does business. This dynamic was enduring, predictable, familiar, and stable across time, consuming time and effort while not curing the financial problems. Ritualistic combat was the norm. The departure of all the offending people in the billing office, the opening of the database, and unilateral disarmament by the billing operation did not change these dynamics significantly. A lack of targets of opportunity, however, eventually led to less combat.

If these dynamics constituted a stable organizational culture or subculture, this case illustrates how difficult, if not impossible, it is to change circumstances like these. When James finally left, many of these CAOs and some of their vice presidents said that James was just like Robert. This justified their behind-the-back attacks and open confrontations with him despite clear evidence to the contrary. They were sure *they* were not the source of the problems. He was.

This story offers some answers to what the purposes of an organization are, implicit as well as explicit. Here group exoneration from culpability (guilt, shame, responsibility) clearly took precedence over billing and collecting for millions of dollars of services (the ostensible task). Put differently, being blameless trumped getting the work done. What keeps the war going? Put differently, why is it so difficult for people to walk away from their persecutory culture? Clearly chronic warfare is part of the unconscious job description. Much of how a company does business is patently irrational and self-destructive.

How can this irrationality and costly destructiveness be understood? First there was the character and role of Robert. He was an experienced head of the billing service. He was highly controlling, and he was answerable to no one but the president. Perhaps he thought he could operate as he wished because he was in a protected position. In particular his control of all the data and information made the president and others dependent on Robert. Much of the effort of the vice presidents, CAOs, and their replacements had been focused on trying to pry information from Robert about what happened to the money they didn't see. Mistrust escalated between Robert and his staff and the vice presidents and their staffs. Even after Robert was fired and replaced by James and his open-book approach, the enmity toward Robert persisted. James was quickly vilified, ultimately described to others as no different from Robert.

It is likely that part of what was occurring psychodynamically was the difficulty of letting Robert go psychologically, of mourning the loss—even of a despised leader. Alexander Mitscherlich and Margarete Mitscherlich (1975) called this "the inability to mourn," a concept that helps us to understand the persistence of mutual recrimination. Although James had tried to institute openness and transparency, he was also seen as a kind of embodiment of Robert. The vice presidents and CAOs and their staffs were too angry to mourn. They would not let go of their many distressing years of experience with Robert.

But what were they angry about? At least in part the anger consisted of displaced and projected guilt from the vice presidents and CAOs onto the billing service for their own denied incompetence. It could be called paranoia. Better to rage against billing than to acknowledge their own flaws. Another dimension of the anger was that the organization was divided into virtual camps, with the "us" group experienced as all good, and the "them" group experienced as all bad. The insider-outsider conflict had become a taken-for-granted part of a long history, and it came to define organizational identity (Diamond, 1993). There was little or no identification with the overall organization and its purpose. An unyielding identity existed only within the members of one's own camp, promoting a very real sense of persecutory transference that assured nothing would change. Millions of dollars were sacrificed in the name of preserving these dynamics. Performance was compromised and income lost—not the most rational of outcomes. Making more money was paradoxically not an option.

STORY 3
THE FIAT

Gary was a new, energetic, ambitious, and charismatic chief executive officer of a midsized corporation. Even before he arrived it was widely known that he would clean house, probably laying off many he did not want. He would then bring in his own people. He almost always got his way in his former position and was a good friend of the president of the board of this corporation. Gary brought in two new division vice presidents, and he was instrumental in the recruitment of a half-dozen senior people from an unrelated industry where they had been stellar performers.

For a while Gary was idolized, and his grand plans were admired. He was generally thought of as possessing the grand vision for the company from which flowed his long-range plans. Everyone else, it seemed, was left to deal with the practical day-to-day stuff and implementing his grand plans. Part of Gary's recruitment style was to promise salary packages and perks, such as secretarial and administrative support, and facilitating promotions. In turn all his new recruits pledged their loyalty to him and their support of his goals. For several years they gave Gary the benefit of the doubt. They were dependent on him and on his presumed adeptness at making things happen.

Gradually they realized that Gary did not, and would not, fulfill his promises. They repeatedly asked for Gary's support, but he kept putting them off and offering reasons why he could not give them additional support or help with their work and promotions. After a while they felt betrayed. Over time they talked with each other and figured out that they were all in the same situation.

At the end of three years they realized that they were in dead end jobs. They felt used, exploited, and condescended to and that they had become mere pawns in Gary's grand scheme. During one three-month period several vice presidents and managers resigned to take positions elsewhere.

Those who remained were shocked and even saddened by the departure of people they knew. They felt impotent to change anything. Some people felt Gary was no hero, only a sham. Others didn't know what to think of Gary anymore. What was happening rapidly gained an epithet, one that was certain to mar the company's reputation. People called it "the exodus" and felt that they had lost good people, hard workers, and dedicated colleagues.

Through this event and for many months thereafter, Gary kept a low profile and reassured the board that all was going well. Those who left had been flawed and needed to go. They were not making the necessary contribution to the bottom line. At a stockholder meeting he buoyantly proclaimed: "When this group left, everyone called it 'the exodus,' as if something were wrong with us. From this day forward we should call it 'the liberation.' Good riddance to them. They did not contribute. They did not fit in. The people who left were not stars but losers. We should be proud of ourselves and not hang our heads in shame. We didn't lose; we won!" Some of those present at the meeting were at first stunned but within a few months saw this historical revisionism as a story about turning the company around. Employees did the same. It was easier to remember it this way.

Questions

How did Gary get away with so much that was ultimately destructive to the corporation?

Why did those who were newly hired, as well as countless others in the organization, accept Gary's vision?

In what ways can Gary be characterized as a charismatic and narcissistic leader?

What is the role of identification with the aggressor in this story?

What is the role of language in this story, and what were its consequences?

Discussion and Analysis

This is an all-too-common story of executive sweet-talking and cunning, arrogance, narcissism, and betrayal. It is a story of command-and-control leadership dependent on the collusion of employees and board members. Gary chose executives, managers, and in some instances employees he could be sure would be dependent upon him (Allcorn, 1992). At the beginning everyone seemed to identify with his charisma and his promise to bring the company to a high level of profitability and national prominence. Gary dazzled everyone with his expansive views for the future. For a while everyone, including board members, basked in the light of his grandiosity. They reflected back to him his greatness and uncritically embraced his promises to make them great and to take care of them. The bitter reality was that he betrayed them and they left.

But Gary still was not finished. With much charm and seeming sincerity he persuaded the board and stockholders that the fault lay with the bad apples, not him. In this story we all have to respect the arrogance, sheer power, and tenacity of an executive who survives a mass exodus and rises from the ashes of his own destructiveness by rewriting history. In a bold move Gary rewrote history by fiat. He arrogantly expected everyone to uncritically accept his historical revisionism. The switch from calling the departure of a large number of key people "the exodus" to calling it "the liberation" magically transmuted loss into gain. Gary's use of language to mask reality is reminiscent of the language of George Orwell's novel *Nineteen Eighty-Four*, with its "Newspeak" and "double-think."

Gary redefined reality. He was able to impose his fantasized reality through his charisma and the desire of others to continue to believe in him and be part of something grand. An outcome such as this may be understood as a defense mechanism known as identification with the aggressor, also referred to as the Stockholm syndrome, which occurs when individuals unconsciously and unwittingly accept the perspectives and actions of a captor, becoming aggressors themselves. Soon those under him would enforce the new reality themselves. Through retrospective falsification a new history solidified Gary's power. The shared fantasy became the new organizational reality, although the events are never fully forgotten, in this case taking some shine off Gary's luster. Eventually many people retreated into their roles and resumed business as usual. It was as though the exodus had never happened.

From a psychodynamic perspective we can imagine that Gary pulled idealizing projections from his employees, board members, and stockholders. Idealizing transference is the companion to the projections that created the fantastic object, in this case Gary the CEO. These projections are then related to past emotions relative to grand constructed figures, creating transference. In this case Gary is loved and admired for his exceptional talents and greatness.

In the long run the idealizing transferences are not sustainable. The initially flawless leader who is the object of projection is ultimately found to be a sham. Idealizing projections and transference are often gradually withdrawn as a result of growing disillusionment, or they may suddenly collapse at some point (for example as a result of a critical event) into a deep hole of despair, disillusionment, rage, disgust, and feeling dirty, used, and alienated. This deep hole is filled with strong emotions that may well have fueled the exodus in the story. Those who left were apparently extremely disillusioned and angry enough to change jobs. They probably felt both that "I have got to get out of *here*" and that "I have to get away from *him*."

STORY 4

UNTOUCHABLES

A president of a university gradually surrounded herself with people who continually flattered her and unquestioningly supported her every decision. These individuals provided her with information about what everyone in the university was saying or doing, thereby allowing her to target people throughout the campus for discipline and not infrequently for termination. She promoted her special staff members one or more times and increased their salaries considerably.

A male CEO, who traveled often with women in various roles, developed serial and sometimes concurrent intimate relationships with some of these women. Many other employees—but not all—knew what was going on. For example a new supervisor who was unaware of the CEO's dalliances with staff members objected to the poor quality and quantity of the work and attendance of one of these employees. The supervisor received an unexpected call from a senior person on the CEO's staff; the message was that the supervisor should leave the employee alone. The supervisor later learned why this had happened.

The chair of a large academic department in a health sciences center has had a long-term relationship with a woman he wants the center to rehire. She was previously forced out of a position at the center for her behavior and poor performance. Her firing was accomplished only with exceptional difficulty because of the chair's connections in the president's office. The chair now says he will pay her salary from his department's budget. However, another departmental chair must rehire her to avoid the perception of a conflict of interest. After interventions by several vice presidents on this chair's behalf, the woman was rehired, to the chagrin of all those who had to work with her previously. However, her role this time is designed to minimize her contact with others.

Yet another example comes from the *New York Times* (Silver-Greenberg, Protess, & Barboza, 2013), which reported that authorities suspect that JPMorgan routinely hired young associates from well-connected Chinese families that ultimately offered the bank business. "Global companies also routinely hire the sons and daughters of leading Chinese politicians. What is unusual about JPMorgan is that it hired the children of officials of state-controlled companies," the *Times* said.

Questions

What is the role of narcissism among executives who designate some staff members as beyond criticism?

How does the creation of untouchable staff affect organizational morale and performance?

What is the role of spying in organizations with untouchable members?

In what ways do organizations with untouchables illustrate organizations with unspoken but widely known secrets?

How does the practice of organizational untouchability affect reality testing in the organization?

Discussion and Analysis

It is not uncommon to find organizations that have staff members who have acquired and keep their jobs in part or entirely because of special circumstances. These individuals often are untouchable in the sense that they cannot be held accountable the way others are. In the public sector political appointees often have a charmed work life; anyone who tries to hold them accountable may be pressured by the mayor, governor, or leader of a major public agency. Likewise, employees often get their job as a result of the influence of a member of Congress or the state legislature, whom the employees may contact if they are not pleased with how they are being treated. The colleagues of these untouchable employees not infrequently see them as reporting directly to this outside individual in a powerful role, creating a very real sense that these untouchables are potential threats to others, including their supervisors.

Interpersonal and organizational dynamics like this are often a product of pathological narcissism. These leaders and executives simply do not think the rules of fair play apply them. The arrogance, omnipotence, and narcissism of power are personified by Louis XIV of France, who supposedly said, "*L'état c'est moi,*"—"I am the state," which also means I am the law, I am beyond the law—meaning there is no higher authority.

Narcissism also contributes to our understanding of the CEO as the primal parent of the primal horde. The CEO in the second example has prerogatives no one else has. He has a coterie of women. Female employees with whom an executive is engaged in multiple relationships sometimes are referred to as comprising a harem, or stable. Other people know this, and the women often know of each other. In one case the wife of the executive took a job in the same organization in order to keep an eye on him.

Group dynamics and fantasies directly or indirectly support the idea that some special individuals in the workplace are untouchable. Others, including superiors, do not challenge the status of these employees, thereby contributing to their job security. These protected, untouchable relationships are invariably publicly known secrets that become taken for granted. When this happens the secrets also become taboo, something that cannot be discussed. This outcome requires organization members to ignore and deny the existence of the special relationships, which in turn leads to individual and shared social defenses that make it important *not* to know what is known. Further compounding the complexity of not knowing is that those with special status promote envy on the part of some who reject the idea of special status for themselves but may also unconsciously wish they had it. This creates internal conflict that these individuals must manage by denying (suppressing) their awareness of the forbidden desire for special status, setting in motion a vicious cycle of being confronted with the special relationships and at the same time trying not to feel envious.

Special and untouchable status may also be intentionally made a part of organizational culture. It is possible to have openly acknowledged and institutionally supported untouchability. This special status becomes more grounded in reality than denied in fantasy. Special status is institutionalized in many ways. One example is organizational skunk works, named for World War II military units (see Peters & Waterman, 2013) that had a special status; they were freed of ordinary organizational roles, rules, and tasks and charged with being creative, coming up with fresh ideas and projects. Yet another example is the pet projects of senior-level executives or CEOs. Such projects become invested with a need to succeed to make the executive look good to others. Put differently, in some instances untouchability may become an institutionalized and well-known good for the organization and its members, who may aspire to join a group with this special status. In this case it may be that what you know is more important than who you know.

STORY 5
SUCH A LITTLE THING

The setting was the weekly division meeting in a department of community medicine in a large urban health sciences center. The division head, Don, a medical doctor, said that he wanted each staff member of his division to interview physicians in the state to determine what topics they felt needed to be researched. Since Joe, a social scientist, was a regular participant at a rural community residency training program two hundred miles to the northeast of Central City, it was natural for him to interview several members of the program's rural community medicine faculty. He undertook this assignment with enthusiasm.

One rural physician, Ed, suggested that research on the treatment of brucellosis be given priority. Rural physicians did not know how to definitively treat brucellosis, a bacterial disease that people usually contract by eating or drinking unpasteurized dairy products. Because it was not a common problem in rural areas, it often went undiagnosed. Joe, recognizing the merit of the idea, made notes about it and said he would advocate for the idea. Another division meeting soon was held. Faculty members, all of whom were physicians except for Joe, presented the results of their interviews. When Joe's turn came, he presented Ed's recommendation that treatment and diagnosis of brucellosis be studied. At the end of Joe's presentation, Don sneered contemptuously and dismissed as "small stuff" the idea of studying brucellosis. Don used the phrase "small stuff" several times in what became an insulting response. He said such research would be inconsequential, would mean little prestige for the department, and would not bring in valued research funding from the National Institutes of Health.

Joe felt that he, Ed, and a few other rural physicians who also thought research on diagnosing and treating brucellosis was important had been ridiculed as useless in the grand scheme of Don's ambition to bring greatness to his division by obtaining large research grants. What was clearly at stake was his personal reputation, not meeting the needs of rural physicians. Even though Joe felt humiliated and the idea had been publicly shamed, he stood his ground, reiterating that rural physicians felt the research would be useful *for them*. Joe had unintentionally become the messenger who is killed, which is common in organizations.

A year or two later Joe learned that the statewide network for practice research had adopted researching brucellosis as one of its projects. The researchers subsequently published papers about this research. Joe, remembering the insult, mentioned this to Don, who strenuously denied that Joe had originally proposed the idea. Rather, Don said, *he* had suggested the idea to nearby physicians within his practice research network, and they had felt that it was indeed a worthwhile undertaking on behalf of all physicians in the region. Joe was astonished at this response. Don said something to the effect that "you had nothing to do with it." The least Don could do, Joe suggested, was acknowledge that he and Ed had initially proposed the subject for research and not rewrite history. Nothing of the sort happened.

Years later, when Don was touting the brucellosis research to illustrate how responsive he was to interests within the network of rural physicians, Joe again mentioned his and Ed's role in proposing the topic for research. Don then modified his account, saying something like, "When you first reported it, I couldn't believe that it had any worth, but when I brought it up to other [urban] physicians, they said that it was a great idea." However, Don was steadfast in not acknowledging that Joe had a role in the inception of the research by initially gathering and presenting the idea.

This was, as Joe remembered, far from the only time in his working relationship with Don that such co-opting of ideas had occurred. Don seemed to be personally invested in not acknowledging Joe (as a non-MD) as the source of any worthy ideas, although this also occasionally happened to others as well. Apparently any idea of merit had to be Don's. This is a phrase often heard in the workplace: "The only good idea is my idea." Don's pursuit of self-enhancement in the moment often led to minimizing the contributions of others to enhance his feelings of self-importance as the final arbiter of what was important. As a result many in the division thought, "Why even bring up a new idea if the idea is going to be disregarded or denigrated?"

Questions

What psychological factors are involved in Don's dismissal and ridicule of Joe's report and, by extension, the suggestions of the rural physician, Ed, whom Joe had interviewed?

Why do you think Don changed his mind about the worth of the study proposed by the rural physicians?

What role might splitting and projective identification have played in this story?

What might be the role of narcissism in this story?

How would you interpret Don's changes in his account of what happened in the story?

Discussion and Analysis

Don did not want to acknowledge that someone else could have a good idea. It seemed that if he could not be the *originator* of the idea, the idea was sheer garbage. Put differently, if the idea had originated with the leader, the leader would have regarded it as brilliant and insightful. But because the source of the idea was someone else, whom the leader arrogantly did not regard as his equal (in Joe's case a non-MD social scientist), the leader had to publicly degrade its worth. In the story Don sees himself as good and omniscient only if he can see Joe and others (perhaps by extension the rural physicians) as bad and as having little or nothing to offer. Don experiences his envy of good ideas that are not his own as distressing and a threat that he must minimize and dismiss so he can maintain his overdetermined pride. Only when other physicians whom Don respected as at least somewhat equal, thereby mirroring him, voiced support for the idea could he affirm its worth, but he also often made it *his* idea.

Organizational and leadership dynamics like this may also be explained in terms of denial, rationalization, and narcissism. In the story Joe did assume a role of being an aversive stimulus, reminding Don where the idea originated. To ignore the contribution of Joe and the rural physicians, Don had to deny it happened or rationalize not remembering it in some way, which is sometimes referred to as selective recall. Joe and Don were together engaged in splitting and projection; each created bad objects (the other) and experienced himself as equal to and even better than the other. This phenomenon also occurs on a vast scale—for example, nationalism. Thus what began as a medical story—a story situated in the institution of American medicine—turns out to be a quite common organizational story, as well as a basis for understanding a world filled with evil nations and empires.

A number of avoidable losses are evident in this story. Joe lost some of his self-respect when he was publicly shamed. Joe also lost respect for Don. And the division lost creative new ideas not only from Joe and the rural physicians but also from those who observed the public ridiculing of Joe's idea. Others thereafter felt uncertain about how their ideas would be received. Touching a hot stove twice is not a good option. Everyone loses in this story.

Yet another aspect of this story is the proverbial killing of the messenger. Joe not only was offended by being killed off (minimized, disregarded, disrespected) but also took offense on behalf of others who were in the same position as he. Joe's feeling of harm might be explained as a narcissistic injury, which is a profound sense of having been hurt. Another element of this dynamic is what happens after someone is killed off. In Joe's case he occasionally would bring to Don's attention his dismissal of an idea that ultimately was proved to be of merit.

And, last, not only in academic circles but in any circumstances, acknowledging that another person is the source of the idea one is using is only civil and courteous. In publishing circles failing to acknowledge this is called *plagiarism*. It is not only unethical but illegal. Joe said that when he told the story about co-opted ideas to another physician-colleague, she quipped, "Plagiarism is the highest form of flattery." Theft as compliment—what a novel idea! But it was also clear Joe could not accept that what had happened was a compliment. It did not feel like a compliment. He felt violated.

STORY 6
IN SEARCH OF GREATNESS

George was a tenured member of the faculty of a college of engineering at a university on the east coast of the United States. He had called Joseph, an organizational consultant and management coach, some weeks earlier and asked for him to come for a consultation. "Joseph, I know too much" were the first words out of George's mouth when they first met in his office. Joseph asked how he could help. The professor responded, "I need someone I trust to know what I know and to certify that I'm not crazy." Joseph said he could not make promises on the latter but that he would be happy to listen to George's story.

The professor began to explain that about five years earlier the university had hired a new dean for engineering, Cecil. "He was touted as the leader we'd been waiting for. He said he would turn this place around and make us a respected college. He was going to bring us out of the doldrums, raise us to national prominence, enhance our reputation, and make us great," George recalled. "One of the first things he did when he arrived was to clean house. He fired almost all the older faculty in administrative jobs and made the lives of the rest so miserable that many voluntarily left. He then brought in his own people."

George continued by saying that he was one of a few original faculty members left. All the new faculty members Cecil had hired were young and relatively inexperienced at teaching and in the politics of academic engineering departments. They were dependent on Cecil because none of them knew how the place worked. For the first few years they thought he could do no wrong. He made them feel they were good and valued faculty so long as they trusted him and let him lead unopposed. He promised the new faculty promotions, salary increases, support staff, and seed money for research. No one dared question him. It was clear he felt he was the only one who knew what was best for the college. If you did not show respect and defer to him, he might humiliate you, making you feel inadequate as a faculty member. Your job might be on the line.

George went on to say that Cecil often traveled all over the country, to Europe, and to oil-rich Arab countries. Cecil said he wanted to see how other schools of engineering worked and raise money as well as look for new faculty. Some of his loyal faculty made excuses for him and asserted that it was the faculty's responsibility to mind the store in his absence. They felt his responsibility was to possess all the vision for the college and search nationally and internationally for ways to fulfill that vision. In contrast the faculty had to work hard for the school "down on the earth." Cecil had the big picture whereas the faculty knew only one class or project at a time. Cecil even had all college stationery printed with "In Quest of Greatness" or "Excellence." The paradox was that faculty members had to believe in their greatness even though Cecil was gradually creating a fiasco; his magnificently envisioned computer system was one example.

Cecil was a technology enthusiast who had committed the college to a vast computer system that would unify the entire college. One day he simply announced the decision to commit millions of dollars to it, and no one questioned it, not even those to whom he reported. He purchased a large number of computers, but he never did provide the necessary leadership to develop the system. The unopened boxes gathered dust in a storage room for a few years, and then one day they all magically disappeared. Nobody said a word. No one dared. And no one seemed to know, even years later, how much money he had wasted on his grand computer system that never happened.

Joseph asked George what was happening within the university at large when Cecil was hired—what was the context? "Interesting question! The university president was just like him!" George explained that the university president, Frederick, had preceded Cecil by about five years. Faculty had begun to call the president Frederick the Great. Charismatic and persuasive, he was an accomplished salesman and sweet-talker. Like Cecil, Frederick first treated people as though they were his best friends. He wanted to know what made you tick. He also often promised that you would be rewarded if you gave him your support. He made you believe that he was really interested in you and that you were the future of the university. Everyone wanted to believe him. He asked the university community to buy in to a new model. Part of his grand vision was that the university would no longer be run by antiquated academic rules that stifled progress. In the future it would be run like a business, *like a corporation.*

Joseph asked George what the outcome of all this was. "You know, Joseph, no one knows exactly what the circumstances were, but Cecil left. Suddenly he wasn't here anymore. We heard rumors of major financial mismanagement, but no one ever sat us down in one place and told us why he left. Cecil just disappeared." George explained that the provost had hired an interim dean, and everyone was supposed to go back to business as usual, as if nothing had happened. But everything around Cecil had seemed to collapse. The university trustees also let Frederick go and without much explanation. The rumor was that he, too, had engaged in questionable financial dealings. George seemed to feel that he was sitting on a story that everyone knew and no one dared discuss. It was all a big secret and crazy making. How could all this happen and then disappear from history?

Now that he had heard the story, Joseph asked George what he could do to help. After all, Joseph was there to consult. George said with a very relaxed face: "*You just did.* You *listened* to my story. You took interest in my experience. You took me seriously. And from the look on *your* face, I don't think that you think I'm crazy. And for all this, I thank you. It really helps."

Questions

What are some of the intended and unintended organizational outcomes when a new leader eliminates most of the leadership of an organization?

How does a new leader bringing in a new team of people affect organization members?

Why does the sudden departure of a leader for no clear reason sometimes go unannounced and not discussed and in the process become a nonevent?

Why is it sometimes hard to talk about missing organization members and leaders?

How important is the role of an attentive and engaged listener in terms of helping others to deal with stressful life and workplace events?

Discussion and Analysis

While this particular story is unique in its details, in its broad dimensions it happens with considerable frequency in the United States and around the world. The story might even trigger readers' memories of similar stories.

This story portrays the world of narcissistic leadership and followership. The leaders and employees in this case were made for each other. They used each other in sad and eventually disastrous ways. Narcissistic executives and employees have an undiscussable emotional contract. For instance a leader promises to make her people feel good if only they will sell their souls to her. This promotes positive and even idealizing transference. Each lives parasitically off the neediness of the other. The leader rewards the unquestioning devotion of the employees. Emotionally needy employees and managers hunger for the leader's affections and affirmation (narcissistic supplies), and the leader hungers equally for their adulation—and submission. This, then, is a group with socially based collusion that must be continually nurtured and defended.

This vicious cycle, perhaps successful in the short run, is disastrous in the long run. In this story both organizational leaders and employees throw reality out the window. They choose to embrace a mutually created world of wish and magic that ultimately fails to hold up in the face of accurate reality testing. Although it is hard to fathom, some people do not know the story, and others—individuals, groups, and even an entire organization with thousands of employees—know it, but they must suppress the knowing from their awareness. Much has been lost, and no one has time to grieve and reconcile. Everyone is merely asked to move on as though nothing has happened.

A final note: In recent decades organizations of all sorts have adopted buzzwords like *greatness* and *excellence*. These words appear virtually everywhere in many forms, such as motivational posters and on letterhead stationery. They are there to broadcast to outsiders the official identity of the organization as conceived by its leader and to rally those who work there to work even harder to make the buzzword the reality. No doubt in many places the attempt is sincere, and the buzzwords express widely (if not deeply) held values. In many others—such as the example from the school of engineering—they are smokescreens and distracters from what is taking place beneath the surface. They are in essence symbols of narcissistic aggrandizement. Not infrequently members of the organization collude in what can become a gradual process of organizational self-destruction.

STORY 7
WHO WILL TAKE THE JOB?

With no warning, the dean, who has just been reappointed, fires the long-serving and effective chair of a major clinical department in a school of medicine. The dean fires several other chairs as well. The dean immediately learns he does not have the resources to recruit new chairs, and the chancellor will also not provide any financial assistance. After a month or more the dean ends up reappointing two chairs to their old positions. However, the chair of the major clinical department rejects the reappointment.

This leads to the appointment of one of the subspecialty division chiefs, Dr. Jones, as interim chair. Under the circumstances the new interim chair proves to be effective. The dean proceeds with external recruiting for a new chair. Predictably the candidates request a recruitment package of space, funding, and positions that the dean does not have. The primary candidate is ultimately enraged when he learns this, since he and his family had traveled to campus a number of times and were starting to negotiate the purchase of a new home. He and all the other candidates reject the dean's substandard job offer.

By now nearly a year has passed. Dr. Jones has performed well as the interim chair. However, he announces that he will leave the department to relocate to elsewhere. When he departs, another division chief, Dr. Smith, is appointed as interim dean. However, he does not want the stressful role and agrees to do it for only one year. One reason the interim role is stressful is that approximately one-third of the faculty has left or plans to leave. None will be replaced until a new chair is appointed. This has left the remaining faculty overcommitted to teaching, research, and patient care.

During this additional year the dean pursues internal recruiting for the chair and targets another willing senior division chief, Dr. Roberts. Dr. Roberts asks the dean for considerably fewer additional resources spread over a longer period of time. Eventually the dean tells him he has to take the role with no additional resources. Dr. Roberts at this point declines the appointment and eventually leaves to take a position elsewhere.

As the second year comes to an end, the interim chair, Dr. Smith, does not agree to continue in the role. The dean at this point has failed to recruit a new chair externally and internally, and none of the remaining division chiefs is willing to accept the role of interim chair. Everyone wonders who will take the job.

This problem proved to be exceptionally resistant to solution. All the likely, and even the less likely, candidates refused the interim role when approached. Eventually even offers to simply be appointed as chair—which under normal conditions would be a highly prestigious position—were rejected. In time a new assistant professor without tenure was identified as someone who would take the position. He was promoted to full professor, given tenure, and became chair of the department.

However, this new chair focused on the status of the role and did not make the important and tough decisions that came with it. Departmental discipline began to break down. He invariably promised resources to everyone who asked, and this overextended the department's resources. The department deteriorated from this point on. Some remaining senior leaders began to leave as well, creating more leadership vacuums.

Questions

Is suddenly announcing a termination without discussing it first a good way to manage organizational change?

How important is it to plan ahead in terms of the resources needed to make a change?

Is it important to build consensus for major leadership changes with the university president and/or the trustees?

How important is it to have a good idea about what can be accomplished with the resources available?

How important is transparency when recruiting, especially senior-level people?

Discussion and Analysis

Events like these undermine the fantasy that rational process dominates organizational life and decision making. Key leaders are fired without considering the systemic effects. Planning ahead for their replacement does not occur. The story also demonstrates that senior leaders can create considerable toxicity that can lead to a near collapse in the operation of large key organizational divisions. In particular ill-considered and erratic leadership can alienate many others who might otherwise step up to provide leadership, leading to a crisis.

The magnitude and extended duration of this problem and process is noteworthy. The fired chair was deeply hurt and so enraged by the sequence of events that he refused reappointment and to work for the dean who had fired him along with two other chairs. Narcissism and arrogance are involved on both sides of this equation. The dean clearly thought he knew best by firing the chairs and did so most cavalierly, then eventually had to backtrack and reappoint the two who would take their jobs back. This had to injure his excessive narcissism and arrogance. As a postscript, this decision ultimately ruined the dean's career in administration, and he had to leave and take a lower-level position at another institution. The chair who refused reappointment also sustained significant harm to his narcissism and feelings of superiority or arrogance. There had immediately emerged a permanent split between the dean and the fired chair that was compounded by the protagonists' splitting and projection. Healing this split was impossible.

The two interim chairs would not continue in the role, with the second agreeing to it only grudgingly in the first place. Few people are willing to assume demanding, high-stress jobs—witness all those who rejected the interim role or appointment as chair. By then contempt for the dean was well established. No one wanted to work for him. He was seen as untrustworthy, thoughtless, and incompetent. The dean was still out for himself, however, trying to look good to others and to solve this problem in any way possible, regardless of its efficacy.

The young assistant professor who eventually accepted the position was enamored of the role and its power and prestige. In addition he did not want to have to hold others to account, and when pressed invariably agreed to do what he was asked in order to avoid making enemies by saying no. He fairly quickly came to symbolize decay and a downward spiral in the department. The loss of about one-third of the faculty remained a hard-to-resolve problem. Neither the dean nor this new chair had the resources to recruit new division chiefs and faculty. Operations continued to unravel.

In the story the dean is repeatedly *self-destructive* as well as destructive of his college of medicine. Perhaps it is no coincidence that he fired an effective chair soon after being reappointed as dean; the reappointment had affirmed his leadership and job security. Self-destructiveness often is rooted in guilt at attaining success. Did the dean have to undermine, even undo, his earlier success? Further, such self-destructiveness has the quality of a repetition—as in a repetition compulsion—of an earlier, even childhood, conflict. If the dean's behavior is a repetition, it is reasonable to wonder what he is repeating.

Finally, the confusion as well as the destruction sown by the dean is impressive. The dean created disarray multiple times and was seemingly unable to learn from experience. Often leaders who create constant uproar in their organizations are externalizing their inner conflicts, so as not to be filled with conflict and confusion themselves. They must see themselves as effective leaders and steadfastly stick to taking action to appear effective, regardless of how ineffective their actions are. In the vernacular they make others crazy to avoid becoming crazy themselves. The group ends up playing out the leader's inner chaotic world and experiencing their world at work as chaotic. In this story many faculty simply left rather than face the chaos.

STORY 8
THE SELL

He was not just another guest speaker. He was a guest of honor. The scene was a special meeting of a school of medicine's primary care clinical department during the 1980's. The department chair had been trying to devise ways to make the department more corporate and in turn enhance its stature among the other academic medical departments in the medical center. The nationally renowned speaker and consultant was addressing many of the clinical departments, hoping to convince them to become more corporate.

The chair introduced the speaker with much fanfare. The chair had required all the physicians in the department, many of them new, to attend this talk. Tom, a tenured basic scientist, was also there and sat and listened to the speaker deliver his talk. The speaker described the medical center and how he envisaged the department would interface with the center and how this relationship building and corporatization would make the department more profitable and competitive.

As the talk continued, Tom realized that a unifying strand was how wonderful those in attendance were, how superb this department was, and how inept and bad other departments, like surgery, were in comparison. The speaker made several comparisons that portrayed the primary care department as looking better than the other clinical departments, which were said to be inept, selfish, unreliable, and possessing other negative qualities.

Tom found himself becoming increasingly ill at ease with this approach. In paying attention to his thoughts and feelings, he was beginning to wonder why he was so upset and angry. He eventually realized that he felt that he and those present were being blatantly seduced. The constant flattery seemed to be leading everyone into a trap the speaker was setting. Tom had a gnawing sense that what the speaker was advocating would hurt the department. When he finished his talk, the audience politely applauded; then the speaker invited everyone to ask questions.

Tom could hardly restrain himself. He was having a strong negative reaction to the speaker and the speech. He raised his hand, and the speaker called on him. Tom spoke simply, saying something like: "Now that you have told this to our department, and made us to look so good, what do you tell other departments about us, about what we are like? You are flattering us in comparison with other departments. Yet you also seek for them to partner with the medical center and become more corporate." The speaker was speechless. The room was dead silent. Tom had drawn attention to the elephant in the room. In order to avoid any further comments from Tom, the chair immediately closed the meeting—not even allowing the speaker to respond.

The speaker was rescued by the chair, who said something dismissive like "This is Tom, and he doesn't understand about these financial things." After the meeting adjourned, several physicians came up to Tom and quietly thanked him for speaking up and confronting the speaker and his not-so-hidden agenda. They also said they had felt uncomfortable during the talk and they were thankful Tom had spoken up for them.

However, by speaking up, Tom had publicly embarrassed the chair by challenging the speaker's agenda for the department. Tom had for the moment called into question the chair's and speaker's corporatizing ambitions. It was clear that the speaker and chair were colluding in their effort to induce the faculty to accept an idea that could transform how they practiced and taught medicine.

Questions

What psychological manipulations occurred in this story?

If you were Tom, what would you have said (or not said) or done (or not done)? What are your reasons?

How did the story make you feel? Put another way, which character(s) do you identify with?

What role(s) do finances, ethics, survival, complicity, and other issues play in the story?

How do you feel about Tom, the chair, the speaker, and the largely
physician audience?

Discussion and Analysis

This is an all-too-common story about the hazards of confronting secret agendas sponsored by the leader that many see but do not respond
to. "The elephant in the room" is a popular expression that speaks to
this dynamic—that a subject is undiscussable, taboo, and that the consequences of violating the taboo are dire. The story is rich in interpretive
possibility. Two taxonomies, or classifications, are useful in interpreting,
if not explaining, the story. First, scholars of drama and opera often identify three common types of characters: heroes, villains, and fools. Second,
the Holocaust scholar Raul Hilberg (1993) identified three characters or
roles common in the human drama of the Holocaust: perpetrators or
executioners, victims, and bystanders. These two frameworks can help us
make sense of the story.

From the viewpoints of the medical center's leadership, the speak-
er-consultant and the chair are heroes but now also heroes temporarily
tainted with a hint of villainy. The faculty had become potential victims
and bystanders seduced into assuming a corporate mentality that would
likely change the nature of their work as physicians.

Tom can be seen as a hero, fool, or villain. When Tom spoke out at
the meeting, he became a temporary hero to many for his courage in
confronting the speaker. Speaking truth to power is always threatening,
and it does take personal courage to do so. The messenger is often slaugh-
tered. Tom can also be seen as a classic fool, the eerie and low-status
character who gives away the whole show and who awkwardly does not
look out for himself. In literature and opera the fool, or jester, is an unas-
suming character that symbolizes common sense and honesty. Notably in
Shakespeare's *King Lear,* the court jester is a character the monarch uses
for insight and advice. The fool takes advantage of his license to mock
and speak freely and by doing so dispenses frank observations that may
even highlight the folly of his monarch. Only a lesser human can do this
and live to speak another day. A greater human who presumes to offer

advice might readily find himself detained in the dungeons or executed (fired). Only by being the lowliest member of the court can the fool, or jester (Tom), become a useful adviser to the monarch.

Tom can also be seen as a villain in the story. By challenging the speaker's integrity and aims, Tom was metaphorically "poking a thumb in the eye" of the chair. Tom's deed was compounded when he publicly humiliated the chair—something that people usually are wise to avoid. Keeping a thin veneer of peace and civility at any price is usually preferable. By speaking up Tom can be seen as a perpetrator and this chair as his victim.

From yet another perspective Tom's exposure of the speaker and of the chair could be understood as an ethical deed rather than an overtly aggressive one. Tom in this case would have felt ethically obligated to speak up. We'll never know. The speaker never did get a chance to respond to questions from the audience. After Tom's intrusive remarks, the chair shut down the rest of the meeting to control the damage.

The six complementary characters used here to discuss the story provide insight into some of its complexity. Who is the hero, perpetrator, or victim? What can be said about bystanders who do not speak up on their own behalf? Understanding the presence, nature, and effects of these roles requires looking at their psychosocial underpinnings.

The story can be understood from psychological and social perspectives. Many faculty who were present were new to the department and inexperienced in university politics. The chair, who had hired them, had promised to look out for them, to nurture their careers, and to take care of them. The unspoken contract with these new recruits was the chair expected fealty in return for taking care of and nurturing them. The chair expected the faculty members to assume roles of dependency and unquestioning loyalty. The unwritten text was that they had to submit to the chair's leadership. During the meeting some present understood that they could not voice what they were thinking and feeling, for reasons of self-protection and survival. Too much was at stake for them in their new careers. The chair held their careers and futures in his hands. As we have noted, speaking truth to power can be dangerous. It could have easily been a career-ending move for them, since everyone knew the chairman was powerful and unafraid to exercise that power.

The mandatory attendance at the meeting also made it clear that this public display of support for the speaker would put the chairman in a positive light. The faculty had been summoned to be present not only to provide applause but also to tacitly participate in an undiscussable collusion that would lead to their being co-opted into going along with corporatization. They could become victims in the process, as their practice of medicine would likely be transformed from valuing patient welfare above all else to valuing profit above patient welfare.

The chair punished Tom by being dismissive of him during the meeting. Over time the chair also reduced departmental support for Tom's work. Ironically both the chair and Tom (and perhaps even the speaker) had been humiliated—a lose-lose-lose outcome. The chair was pursuing his own self-aggrandizement by flattering the speaker with a receptive audience. Tom spoke to the reality principle and the elephant in the room. Tom's comment called into question the motivations of the speaker, the chairman, and their slick presentation, publicly humiliating the speaker and by doing so torpedoing the chair's plan for a receptive audience. The faculty, who were largely bystanders, implicitly became losers as well. By assuming a passive role relative to the chair's desire to make the department more corporate, they probably would compromise the teaching and patient care that they so highly valued.

From a psychodynamic viewpoint Tom found himself in a role unilaterally imposed on him by the chair—the person (fool) who does not understand the importance of making money. This role included splitting and projective identification. Tom had provided the chair with projective hooks. He was a thoughtful and reflective scientist who did not generate clinical income for the department from treating patients, bringing in only the occasional research grant.

Tom, it may be speculated, may well have incorporated some of the chair's projections as being worthless to him and the department, a process that is known as "introjective identification." The act of taking over another person through projective identification is an act of violent interpersonal aggression. It is *soul* murder. When the chairman forcefully projected and Tom introjected the projection, Tom became a "false self" (Winnicott, 1965) who has lost or repressed his "true self" along the way. Thereafter Tom may well unwittingly come to feel worthless, as the chair desires, and by doing so may relieve the chair of this unwanted self-experience because he has placed it in Tom. The chair then may safely denigrate this "deposit" as an act of projected self-hatred carried out in another person—Tom.

Tom showed how, in being "himself," he also voluntarily assumed a role for the chair and the group, that of calling into question the not-so-hidden agenda for the meeting. Tom, as himself, carried something valuable and dangerous for the group, becoming what is called a projective vessel. Some could value him disproportionately (positive transference) or similarly disproportionately devalue and even despise him (negative transference).

And, finally, if Tom was the object of transference from the chairman and the group, what was his own transference? Perhaps for Tom the chair represented paternal authority, a man who used his power to abuse and violate his "children," the members of his department who were his "family" and emotionally and financially dependent upon him. Clearly as the leader the chairman had all the power implicit in the role of father, and he used the power in this role to metaphorically castrate Tom.

Story 9
Hit List

An executive who headed a research division within a large division of a much larger department asked the recently hired department administrator to promote a member of the executive's staff. Because the context was a bureaucratic structure that included a department of human resources, the administrator asked the executive to supply a revised job description to support the request. Once received it would be sent to human resources for review.

A few days later the executive strode into the administrator's office. He was clearly angry and agitated. He walked up to the administrator's desk and stood there, looming over the administrator. *How dare* the administrator ask him for a revised job description? The executive proceeded to explain why the administrator's behavior was inappropriate.

A minute into his explanation, the executive stopped and said aloud, "This is not going to work." After a short pause he launched into a second statement with the same result, saying aloud he could not argue by analogy. After a moment he began a third statement. Once again he stopped partway through it. He stood there for a moment without saying anything. Suddenly, still infuriated, he turned around and walked out of the office. During this entire episode the administrator never said a word. He had simply listened intently to the monologue.

A week later the administrator received the revised job description he had requested, and the staff member eventually was promoted. The administrator learned from another member of the division that the executive was so enraged by the administrator's behavior that he had added the administrator to his "hit list." This list included other names and would, everyone expected, soon be put to use when the executive was appointed a vice president. The administrator and others would then be forced to leave or would be terminated shortly after he was promoted.

Questions

In what ways does the story illustrate organizational bullying?

How did the administrator respond to the executive's bullying?

What are the psychological purposes of the department executive's "hit list"?

What is the role of flight from reality in this story?

In what ways does this story illustrate narcissism?

Discussion and Analysis

A story like this speaks to the psychological nature of the workplace where things have gone wrong. Initially the executive felt insulted at having his will challenged by a mere administrator. The executive clearly wanted not to be questioned. Anyone who did so might be added to the hit list and eventually attacked. This dynamic speaks to an excessive sense of self-entitlement and inflated self-importance on the part of the executive, one often described with such terms as *narcissistic, arrogant,* and *vindictive.* Even though the administrative request was entirely reasonable and necessary to achieve the requested outcome, clearly merely asking for the job description resulted in the expression of nearly uncontrolled and uninhibited rage.

The executive's anger was compounded by his multiple attempts to explain logically why he did not have to comply. The self-editing eventually increased his sense of frustration at being unable to impose his will in the moment, resulting in even more rage at failing to meet his own self-expectations to be logical. That the administrator never said anything was lost in the moment.

When he became a vice president, the executive forced the administrator out of the company. This speaks to narcissistic injuries, expansive and arrogant but also fragile pride, and feelings of inflated self-importance that, if called into question in any way by anyone, will have to be vindicated. Individuals like this almost never forget such injuries. Those who inflict these injuries end up on a hit list for life. Vindication and revenge are often, if not always, sought, and others know this from experience and observation. The executive becomes feared not only because he feels highly offended when he thinks someone has crossed him but also because he will use the power of his position to remove the offending individual.

Some people in the workplace cannot bear to be wrong—especially in another's eyes—even when they *are* wrong. They may seldom, if ever, admit a mistake. The shame they feel is too acute and overwhelming. Sometimes they can come up with a coherent verbal rebuttal and vindicate themselves in the moment. The executive in this story could not do so, creating a real sense of inflamed rage relative to his narcissistic wound of shame, which was unintentionally inflicted by the administrator. Who would *dare* question him? For the executive, and others like him, the only solution imaginable is to obliterate the person who is the source of the injury. The unconscious goal is to be forever *invisible* to the person who exposed him to shame by getting rid of him.

Also to be considered is that if this executive had been in a lesser role, as he was initially, he would have lacked the power to remove the administrator. This would have led to a different approach to self-vindication, such as continually undermining the administrator's work and credibility. In this instance the executive who became a vice president had the authority and power to make his fantasy of annihilating the administrator a reality. Forcing the administrator to leave eventually compensated for the intense narcissistic injury he felt the administrator had inflicted on him, in addition to removing him as a reminder.

Events like this are unfortunately all too common in the workplace. Organization members come to know who is dangerous and will use their power to lay waste to others, who often unintentionally offend them by simply doing their job. Recent attention directed to organizational bullies underscores the presence of this unfortunately unchecked organizational violence.

STORY 10

THE SETUP

The dean of a medical school one day received an unexpected bill during a meeting with the new teaching hospital's CEO, Thomas. Thomas had been hired to improve the hospital's financial situation; for the past few years it had been running in the red and draining the university's resources. During the meeting Thomas handed the dean a letter saying that the hospital was going to start billing the medical school for all the building maintenance services the hospital had been providing to the school. He also gave the dean a twelve-inch pile of bound reports to support the billing.

The dean was incredulous. Thomas had begun to swamp the dean with lengthy reports to justify taking various unilateral actions relative to the school. In this case, in addition to the changed relationship with the hospital, the medical school would now be expected to absorb a bill of more than $1 million for maintenance.

The dean contacted a consultant who was working on several projects for him and asked the consultant to provide him with advice. The consultant took the pile of reports to his temporary office. The reports were vast and listed every pump, valve, pipe, electrical panel, and much more in the seven-story medical school building. The report included the cost of maintaining each of the many thousands of items listed.

The consultant's next step was to contact the employee, Beth, who was responsible for generating the detailed report. A meeting was arranged. During the cordial meeting Beth proved to be informed about the report and its data. The consultant asked a few questions about identification numbers, locations, and equipment descriptions. Beth had the answers. The consultant then asked about the associated costs, which presumably included both maintenance and replacement costs. As the questioning proceeded, Beth ultimately could not answer how, exactly, the costs had been determined, and she acknowledged this. She said she would research it and phone with the answers. The next day she did call, reporting that she had found a more detailed report of cost determinations.

Once again the consultant met with Beth and reviewed the new report, but the result was the same. No matter how specific the numbers were, Beth could not say how, exactly, the numbers had been arrived at and said that she saw no further way to break the costs down. She left to research this further and phoned the next day. After interviewing a number of staff members who had contributed to the cost-determination report, Beth reported that the numbers were actually fictitious—they were, she said, "best guesses." There was no particular logic to them, although the massive reports implied a clear rationale in developing them. They certainly did not constitute a reasonable basis for paying out $1 million in maintenance costs. Beth had nothing further to say.

The consultant reported to the dean that, despite the volume of numbers and vast listing of line items, the cost basis was basically fabricated cost numbers. The dean then refused the CEO's request for payment, saying until he received concrete cost determinations using industry standards, he would not consider the matter further. The consultant subsequently learned that within a few days of the dean's response, Beth had been fired.

Questions

Why did the new CEO have the financial reports confabulated?

How did Beth, in doing her job, inadvertently reveal organizational secrets or taboos?

Why do many organizations sacrifice some of their own members?

What is the relationship between a CEO's grandiosity and the psychological response of the group (employees)?

How often are proposals grounded in incomplete, inaccurate, and partially distorted information that is then used to make a rational argument?

Discussion and Analysis

Thomas and the executives above Beth who commissioned and presumably reviewed the report before it was handed over as a bill had to have had some idea that the numbers were made up or, if not, they should have known. From the start all hospital executives behind the report stood to lose face if someone in the school checked it out. And of course Beth forthrightly and with some innocence revealed the truth behind the seemingly well-documented reports. Beth had, however, crossed the executives by revealing the truth, and she was rewarded by being fired. Without knowing it, Beth had become a whistleblower. Her sense of honesty and responsibility set her up to fail and to be sacrificed as a scapegoat. Truth telling, she learned, had its risks.

It seems clear in the story that the new CEO decided to improve the hospital's financial condition at the expense of the medical school and its dean, who was not very well prepared to examine and refute the reports and analysis that Thomas said supported shifting costs to the medical school. Firing Beth also amounted to killing the messenger. Sacrificing workplace scapegoats is so common as to be taken for granted. In this story Beth's firing provided cover for Thomas and his colleagues. Saving face is sometimes more important than anything else in organizations. By terminating Beth, Thomas and his staff were making two things clear. They would be willing to sacrifice others in order to keep their jobs, and crossing them in any way was a potentially career-ending decision. The hospital executives might very well stop at nothing in order to look good and effective. Psychodynamically speaking, they constituted an amalgam of narcissism and a willingness to do the wrong thing and act unfairly in a predatory fashion.

In particular it is common to find CEOs and senior executives who appear to be bigger than life and quite powerful. In part this is associated with the positions or roles that they occupy. It is also the case that they are often held in high regard and feared as a result of splitting and projection on the part of the employees, who, by projecting their personal sense of power, confidence, and importance onto these leaders, leave themselves depleted and with the self-experience of being diminished, ineffective, dependent, and weak compared to the powerful and admired executives.

The theme of the sacrifice of scapegoats also merits further exploration. This happens in organizations all the time. For instance some army privates were held responsible for abusing prisoners in Iraq, when it was also a chain-of-command problem. In contrast, whistleblowers intentionally pull the temple down on their heads. As the consultant experienced it, Beth was trying to answer his questions in good faith. She did not know the numbers were fabricated until she researched their derivation. And to her credit she was not prepared to lie.

An additional element of the story is that the CEO was trying, subtly or not so subtly, to bully the dean by generating huge reports that he knew the dean could not evaluate and did not have the staff to do so. Eventually the CEO had to abandon this strategy, at least in the case of the $1 million bill and likely thereafter, because the dean had learned that he could not necessarily trust that Thomas was making an honest request—that what the CEO asserted was supported by detailed but also accurate and truthful documentation.

STORY 11
THE JEW IN THEIR MIDST

Ken is a new and ambitious academic medical researcher who has been hired to transform an institute into a regional network with national prominence. He supervises Jerry, a tenured member of the faculty who works at the institute as a social scientist. Ken does not think social science is real science, and he is strongly opposed to Jerry's work and even to his presence at the institute, despite Jerry's track record as an accomplished social science researcher who is nationally recognized in his field. Ken often publicly degrades Jerry and his work, occasionally also humiliating him in private. Although Jerry's ostensible job description is to serve as an applied sociologist on R&D projects, Ken forbade him to use concepts like culture or society in his work because "nobody will understand you." Ken dictated the language of discourse the social scientist was permitted to use. Ken often said to him: "You've published a lot, but very few people in the field can understand what you're saying. . . . You keep asking for respect, but you don't deserve any. . . . You've received numerous national awards for your work, but they are given by the wrong organizations. Don't you understand that they don't count around here?"

Paradoxically some ideas of Jerry's that Ken publicly ridiculed Ken later adopted as his own in projects, grant applications, and publications. On one occasion Ken temporarily softened and confided to Jerry that maybe he was bit envious of him. Ken mentioned he always wanted to be a field and stream biologist, not a hard-driving medical researcher and administrator responsible for an institute. "I look at you and I see what I'd like to be: here's a guy who does what he likes and doesn't listen to anyone." This was an exaggerated characterization, but Jerry was also known to often speak up in meetings to raise other perspectives that sometimes challenged those Ken was putting forward. Ken made it clear he would like to have a job description that would allow him to devote 50 percent of his time to writing and publishing and not be burdened by all his responsibilities as director of the institute. In saying this, Ken was in the moment creating a fictional (projective) character (Jerry), whom he then envied but also punished.

On a later occasion, while Jerry was driving Ken to a meeting at another site, Ken lectured Jerry about the nature of Jerry's problem and then offered to help him:

What is it with you Jews? You act just like the other Jews I've known. I've never been able to understand why you act as if you're so special. Look at the history of the Weimar Republic before Hitler came into power. Jews were overrepresented in government, in the arts, in science, in medicine, in the media, in everything. They were in control of the whole country. Can't you understand why Germans wanted to get rid of them, to get their own country back?

It seems to me like the Jews bring persecutions upon themselves. I know it's terrible to say—and I'll deny that this conversation ever took place if you say anything about it—but the Jews push their way into everything. What happened to them was horrible, but much of it owes to their own doing. It's the same here in America. Jews have infiltrated the government, the news media, the arts, science. They want to control everything.

And you're just like them. You act as if everyone is against you. It is not true. You get surprised when we push back. I don't know how to get you to realize that I'm on your side. You just need to downplay your writing projects in the home office. You've got to realize that few medical and bioscience researchers can understand your papers. Your future here at the institute depends on your ability to be less rigid and to trust me.

Jerry was astonished by this lecture. He felt humiliated, enraged, and impotent to do anything. He haltingly tried to explain himself to Ken, who seemed to Jerry to be emotionally frozen—hard as a rock. Jerry felt cornered and trapped and remembered driving the rest of the way to their destination in silence. He, the Jew, had suddenly become a big problem that could, it seemed, be remediated only by not being Jerry, Jewish, and even present.

Questions

In what ways is Ken's management style toward Jerry one of bullying?

What were Jerry's emotional responses to Ken's bullying?

What might be some of the psychodynamics underlying Ken's bullying?

What role might projection play in this story?

What role might Ken's perception-stereotype of Jerry's ethnicity play in this story?

What role does reality testing play in this story?

Discussion and Analysis

This story illustrates the operation of nationalistic and totalitarian thinking that could arise in any workplace. It shows how mundane, but also offensive, organizational fascism can be. The story entails a conflict between a powerful director of a research institution (Ken) and a Jewish social scientist (Jerry) working in the institute. The social scientist is known to be independent and often expresses dissenting views in workplace meetings, in addition to researching and writing in a field rejected as not-science by many biomedical researchers. Ken, who liked to maintain tight control of his projects and workers, regarded Jerry as a loose cannon for his willingness to offer divergent opinions and ideas and as a loser in terms of his field, research, and publishing. Jerry was, psychologically speaking, a bad Other, or object, that Ken thought he needed to control, minimize, or even dispose of, at least in fantasy.

Much of Ken's perception of Jerry was governed by splitting and projection that blurred and violated interpersonal boundaries and, more fundamentally, represented an invasive assault on who Jerry was. Jerry could eventually come to know himself as simply bad relative to Ken and his colleagues—a nuisance and worthless contributor to the institute. When splitting and projection occurred in this instance, Ken may also be understood as trying to control a bad part of himself that he had located in Jerry. These bad and undesirable aspects of self are, in one's mind, split off from oneself and located in another through projection. And to the extent that Ken wanted Jerry to experience himself in a way consistent with Ken's projections, Ken would expect Jerry would come to know himself to be the way Ken wanted. Ken would treat Jerry as though he were that way, encouraging Jerry to see himself that way. Jerry would, if this occurred, become alienated from himself and his identity as a social science researcher and as a Jew, an outcome sometimes referred to as false self and projective identification.

Jerry could be understood to have come to embody what Erik Erikson (1968) spoke of as the "negative identity," that is, the condensed image of all one rejects about oneself and one's internal representations. What Ken had to disown and repress in himself he projected into Jerry (and others), who came to embody much of what Ken could not be, wanted to be, and even envied in others who were not oppressed by a major managerial role. In the abusive diatribe in the car, what Ken ultimately offered to Jerry was a protection racket that would require Jerry to sacrifice his personal integrity. In return for Jerry's promising to not be himself, Ken would offer to protect Jerry by not attacking him in the future.

Even more fundamentally alienating was that Jerry had become "the Jew," a stereotype rather than a person. Ken saw Jerry as a threat, just as he saw Jews as ever-present threats. Hypernationalist (Nazi) stereotypes and xenophobia played a role in Ken's perception and experience of Jerry. The language Ken used during the trip in the car points to the presence of unconscious dynamics and deeply ingrained fears instilled by social-ization. These and other undiscussable dynamics contributed to the strife that existed between Ken and Jerry.

There is a broad point to be made. The American workplace is be-coming ever more diverse and filled with different nationalities, religious groups, and cultural heritages. Everyone increasingly has to work with many different kinds of people. Differences in ethnicity, religion, gen-der, region, and professional alliances are changing the character of the workplace in the United States and around the world. Ideals of diversity that include interdisciplinary research collaborations are challenging tra-ditional ideas of workplace homogeneity and hierarchies. In the story this is illustrated by Ken's not understanding Jerry as a person, colleague, social scientist, or as a Jew. Ken made little effort to see the world through Jerry's eyes. He took the easy path of simply fearing and rejecting what he did not know, condemning Jerry to a workplace filled with an eternity of rejection. Jerry's experience is, then, much like that of millions of differ-ent Others in workplaces.

Individual and group differences that are not well understood promote uncertainty, sometimes fear, and always anxiety, leading to reliance on psychological defensiveness. This can then degenerate into seeing these different Others based on stereotypes, projections, and some degree of unfounded certainty that these Others are defective objects and a threat. These types of interpersonal, group, and organizational dynamics can provoke an exceptional level of arrogance and narcissism, many times fu-eled by leaders who, by their actions, propagate these outcomes through-out the workplace. In the story it was clear that Ken felt himself to be the final judge of who was acceptable and what type of research and publish-ing was of value. His arrogant and absolute certainty put Jerry and others in impossible positions.

Speaking out against this can be a career-ending decision. Any attempt to take issue with what managers and supervisors say and do can elicit a strong defense and punitive response, creating an interpersonal context of dominance-submission: I win, you lose. Ken perceived disagreement with him (something that nicked his arrogant self-pride) as confirmation of the stereotype: "You see, by challenging what I said, you are making my point. You think you know everything."

In saying this Ken not only traps Jerry but also, it must be appreciated, is trapping himself within the context of his certainty about Jerry, created in part by ignoring who Jerry is and steadfastly adhering to a view of Jerry created by projections and the imposition of stereotypes. Only if Ken takes the time to put down his anxiety-driven defenses relative to Jerry and get to know him for who he really is can Ken grow as a person in a workplace role. Only by doing this can those who act this way liberate themselves and those around them to be themselves, and more accepting of individual differences, allowing for the development of interpersonal understanding and connectedness.

STORY 12

TOMBSTONE

A research organization succeeded in hiring a top-flight scientist, Robert, in an area where leadership was needed. Before he began work, he supervised long distance the renovation of his future lab, including the purchase of the equipment and supplies. When he arrived at the lab, renovations were finished and the equipment and supplies were in boxes. Almost immediately he began a long, obsessive process of criticizing the renovations and space in the area of the building where the lab was located. Much effort and additional funds were put into responding to these many criticisms. It seemed that nothing and no one could please him.

During this start-up period he hired a secretary and a new lab technician. He also arranged to have a position for a colleague, Tim, whom Robert brought with him. Within the first three months the new secretary left to take a position elsewhere. The new, experienced female lab tech began to visit the lab administrator, Shawn, to complain about how Robert was treating her. She reported him as being hypercritical of her and her work, sometimes verbally abusive, and not infrequently demeaning. She met with Shawn a few more times, and Shawn offered to help her find a new position. She left within three months. During this period Tim had to be admitted to a mental health facility and remained a medicated psychiatric outpatient thereafter.

A new secretary and lab tech were recruited. And after a few months both were visiting Shawn to report a variety of abusive interpersonal and supervisory behavior. At this point Shawn had become familiar with many stories about Robert in addition to his (Shawn's) first-hand experiences. The senior research executive in charge of the facility was not willing to confront and perhaps alienate Robert and eat the cost of the considerable investment made to recruit him. As a result Shawn was left with the only alternative of once again offering help in finding a new position for the technician, and she, too, was gone within a few months. The secretary, Diane, also visited with Shawn to report how she was treated. Diane eventually spoke of having been physically and emotionally abused by her husband for many years, and she said she did not need two men in her life like this. She, however, remained in her position for many years.

Shawn recruited a third lab technician, Andy, an older PhD with many years of experience. After a few months Shawn stopped by to see how things were going. Andy spoke positively about the work and made a point of avoiding saying anything further. Less than a year later police informed Shawn that Andy had been found dead, leaning up against a tombstone in a cemetery in another state—a suicide.

Questions

How can a destructive leader be identified early in his employment? What prevents such identification?

How can repetitive patterns of abuse be identified and stopped?

Can qualities in a leader initially thought to be assets ultimately be recognized as liabilities?

What are some impediments to the recognition, by upper management and boards of directors, that they exercised poor judgment in selecting a leader?

How can upper management and boards of directors prevent disastrous hiring decisions such as for Robert?

Discussion and Analysis

This senior research scientist, Robert, developed conflict-ridden relationships with employees, and he invested a lot of time and energy into opposing and maligning his staff and Shawn. He bullied and criticized people, handing out caustic criticism as though he were the final judge of everything.

Robert's behavior is not all that uncommon in the workplace and may be exceptional only when viewed for its extreme nature. There are endless stories about people in positions of power and authority who denigrate, publicly humiliate, minimize, threaten, bully, and otherwise harm individuals and groups. This is the stuff of good Hollywood and TV series drama. The characters offer up outrageously antisocial behavior and by doing so become cult figures and antiheroes. Unfortunately these characters and plots seem most often to have been ripped from newspaper headlines after the same behavior becomes newsworthy.

In Robert's case he continually chased away staff until some people were hired who, while not liking their treatment, sometimes tolerated it because it was a familiar theme throughout the rest of their lives. Having a problem like codependency (Allcorn, 1992) often means that someone stays loyal to an abusive other, who may be an alcoholic, drug abuser, or sufferer of a clinical psychological disorder such as pathological narcissism and antisocial disorder.

In order to maintain attachment and not suffer loss of attachment and employment, the codependent person is willing to submit to almost anything. Codependent people have difficulty learning from experience and from an observer's perspective tend to repeat abusive, degrading relationships in most areas of their lives. People often psychologically transfer unconscious conflicts and relationships from childhood and marriage to the workplace, and by doing so they reenact familiar life dramas in unfamiliar places, thereby making them familiar.

Robert's behavior, given its high level of interpersonal toxicity, might be understood to be psychopathic or subclinical psychopathy. Malignant narcissism might also explain why he had to control and dominate others, trying to make them submit to his dominance. Ultimately we are left to stand in awe of this intensely abusive behavior and wonder why—and how—outcomes such as Andy's suicide might be prevented.

Although we are probably outraged at stories like this, organizations often hire division heads and other leaders because they look like, and present themselves as, exactly what the organization needs. What later shows up as psychopathic arrogance appears at first to be ambition and confidence. Antibullying policies and abuse-prevention programs can hardly succeed where the personality of the leader is an emotional fit for boards of directors, trustees, and regents who prize ambition, excellence, productivity, and profit at any cost. Trustees who seek to lead their organization by hiring change agents are often attracted to leaders who speak with confidence, offer up grand ideas, and have a track record of making tough personnel decisions that lead to organizational downsizing and restructuring. Aggressive, tough-talking leaders regrettably sound, to many board members, like they are just right.

Conclusion

If they do anything, these stories illustrate the close connection between destructive leaders, leadership, and the darker side of organizational life that can be toxic to individuals, groups, and the organization as a whole. Failure, waste, conflict, self-centered pursuits, not being held accountable, scapegoating, manipulation, bullying, threatening, and intimidation can be transformative and life changing or even life ending. In providing these stories, along with discussion and analysis, we hope we have encouraged critical reflection and perhaps a sense of not being alone in having had such experiences. You are not alone, and certainly the inability in many instances to fend off these experiences is not new either. The latter is not a sign of weakness or ineffectiveness and certainly should not be experienced as shame. Escaping to another job and risking a repetition is not always a good option. We are, it seems, left with the hardest question of all: What can we do?

We have no easy answers. Our efforts here are directed at reflection, critical thinking, and acquiring knowledge and insight that can be put to use in a process of appreciating leader behavior and organizational dynamics. Understanding how to use a psychodynamically informed approach offers many insights into leader and follower behavior as well as group and organizational dynamics. In our view this is essential in terms of maintaining personal integrity while staying connected to accurate reality testing that can, as the stories illustrate, reveal a dark, if not depressing, organizational landscape. This knowing and appreciation are a first step toward maintaining personal integrity and surviving in these organizational landscapes. In part 3, informed by all the stories, we provide more thoughts on what can be done.

We now turn our attention to the interaction of followers relative to leaders and leaders relative to followers. This perspective emphasizes the interactive nature of leader and follower dynamics as well as group dynamics, which are often shaped by out-of-awareness and undiscussable psychodynamics.

CHAPTER 5

Projection and Organizational Crazy Making

Introduction

The workplace is filled, we argue, with splitting, projection, and transference that are sometimes hard to spot and at other times all too evident. These dynamics can be intensely imposed and last for years or for only a few fleeting moments. The stories in this chapter speak to this dynamic from a number of perspectives. Sometimes leaders are paralyzed by perceived and real threats and in a sense are made to feel crazy by what is going on around them and the nature of the projections and transference onto them. These projections can become, if integrated (through projective identification), transformative, changing how leaders know and experience themselves and others. Something as simple as their position or title can draw projections and transference consistent with encounters employees had with people who held similar titles in the past or with fantasies employees had about a person with such a title.

This dynamic need not be limited to projection onto leaders with authority and power. Others in the workplace may also be subjected to projection by leaders, as well as by their friends and colleagues. This is especially true not only with respect to minorities and women who are treated as objects but also with respect to age and other personal or social attributes. This appreciation is underscored by the final story in this chapter, the dynamics of which can be readily understood as crazy making.

We remind readers that these are stories that actually happened and may also be familiar in some personal ways to many readers. We have provided a list of thought-provoking and reflective questions after each story, and we encourage you to take a moment to ponder before continuing to the discussion and analysis.

STORY I
THE CHANGE

Joe was definitely making a success of his career as an administrative manager. Now in a new organization, he expected he would be able to apply all his experience and skills to an organization that needed better management. The position had the title of vice president for finance and administration, and it was a new position in the organization.

Soon after he started work, he noticed his colleagues were treating him much differently from how colleagues had treated him in his old job as a manager at his former organization. Since this was a new position in the organization, and Joe was new to the organization, he was struck by a consistent phenomenon: people seemed to "know" him. The knowing seemed to be linked to his job title, which included finance.

Joe knew from experience that it would be fair to say that many executives in exclusively financial roles try to control just about everything about finances, and even operations that are dependent on budgets approved by the chief financial officer (CFO). This, he knew, was not so much a stereotype as a reality. Joe, however, usually went out of his way to avoid using his control of financial matters to control sections within the larger organization. Nonetheless, as he worked, others invariably seemed to already know him. It seemed that, in their minds, he and the stereotype were one and the same. They were ignoring evidence to the contrary.

A typical example of an interaction that had this stereotype embedded in it was an opening discussion with Joe by several executives who wanted to purchase new equipment. From the start these executives assumed Joe would not be receptive and would withhold the necessary funds. They began their presentation anxiously and defensively, and as it progressed they became angry about what they expected would be a refusal of funding or even any reasonable consideration of their request. By the time they were finished, they appeared to be defeated. However, to their surprise, Joe was open to considering their ideas. He did, however, ask for more information about the proposal and its costs and volunteered to help them do this work. Nonetheless the request fulfilled their worst fears about being rejected, and they clearly did not want to do the work to make the proposal sound. Double binds like this are an essential part of financial management—yes, but.

Questions

How important is it to consider how people will see you in a new position?

Is it possible to manage how people see you and treat you in a management role?

Why are some management roles associated with stereotypes, and how do they influence the person in the role?

How likely is it that a person in a management role will become more like the projected stereotype?

Is it ever entirely possible for the person in a role to fulfill unrealistic expectations of others?

Discussion and Analysis

That no one knew Joe and that the position was new were facts. Joe, however, almost immediately found himself viewed with suspicion, sometimes with fear, and occasionally with contempt. Although he steadfastly avoided fulfilling other employees' worst fantasies, others nonetheless were certain they knew him, or at least how he would behave as a financial executive. This level of certainty is sometimes referred to as pathological certainty, when all evidence to the contrary is steadfastly ignored (selective attention). Joe is guilty and can never be proved innocent of acting like the stereotype of a financial executive. In the eyes of others he simply becomes nearly all bad—the punishing, withholding, manipulative CFO. This all-bad persona is in large part the product of splitting and projection. Others split off the parts of themselves that are like the stereotype and project them onto Joe, who in turn admittedly provides projective hooks, one of the most prominent of which is the job title with *finance* in it, and the request in the story for more information. Dynamics like these are also fueled by the transference of past feelings to the present, the result of feelings that arose from such things as not receiving nurturance as a child or young adult or failure to receive a better office, promotion, or raise as an employee. Confrontations with authority figures who unilaterally control resources often are filled with some level of transference. The individual is split apart in someone's mind to become largely all bad.

Once projection takes place and pathological certainty develops, everyone who enters Joe's office feels he is a threat. In this story they expect him to be a person who will withhold financial resources, thereby killing the project or idea they had in mind. Along with this sense of what will happen, they transfer to the present past negative emotions about being rejected and having resources withheld. They not only know what Joe will say and do, they already hate him for this. Unless Joe can gradually succeed in reversing all these projections and the accompanying transference to him, he will be stuck with them so long as he is in the position.

Also to be considered is this: if Joe was not like the projections at the beginning, the constant press of the projections onto him might result in his internalizing them. By identifying with the projections, he gradually comes to see himself as like the projections and how people are treating him. In essence, if everyone thinks he is this way, he may well be this way. The projections become experienced as his attributes. As a result, if he is not careful, he may well simply become like the fantasized CFO and lose those parts of himself that were not like this when he started the new job. Joe can become the fantasized CFO monster (projective identification). What does he have to lose by becoming the monster, since nothing he does staves off the projections and transference?

STORY 2
BECOMING A FIGMENT OF OTHERS' IMAGINATION

Early in his career Steven, a Jew, and his wife, Gretchen, attended a company Christmas party. The head of the medical research division, Robert, introduced them to a number of those gathered. One introduction that caught Steven's attention went something like: "This is Steven, my bastard son, and his lovely wife, my daughter, Gretchen." Robert smiled; his gambit was supposed to be humorous, with the intent of disarming any anger Steven might have toward its inappropriateness. After all, it was all in fun. However else one might interpret the idea of "bastard son," it inescapably implied that Steven was illegitimate, if not as a person then certainly as a scientist conducting research in a not-well-accepted area in the company.

This was unexpected because the two were collaborating on several major projects and had seemingly become close friends. Who Steven was as a man, a researcher, and as a Jew did not appear to be a problem (at least initially). He and Robert seemed to have a comfortable level of accepting each other. However, with time a clear undertone of suspicion and doubt as to who the other was had developed.

For example, Steven was responsible for organizing the Friday noon conferences for the medical research division. He had contacted people in the wider community to speak on topics related to his area of specialization but branched out into other areas of interest within the division. For the first year or so Robert insisted that Steven discuss with him each prospective topic and speaker. Robert half-jokingly said a number of times that he wanted to be sure Steven did not bring in unacceptable speakers or individuals with radical ideas to influence the other researchers. In particular Robert said he was worried Steven would bring in radicals from the northeastern United States who might contaminate and offend the sensibilities of the researchers, who were primarily from southern states. After about a year or so Steven passed the politics test. He could plan his conferences without first getting Robert's approval. He was safe. He felt he was on the way to being accepted and becoming one of "us" rather than remaining one of "them."

Robert also had some clear ideas about why Steven and Gretchen had chosen to live where they did. "I bet I know why you chose to live in Jericho," Robert said one day. "I bet when you heard the name, you thought that it would be a Jewish community since it is a town from the Old Testament." Once again caught off guard, Steven responded that his sister-in-law and her family were living there and that his wife and he enjoyed spending time with them and wished to live reasonably close to them.

One of Steven's best friends and staunchest supporters was John, a colleague from a rural town. Over the years he had helped to keep Steven's spirit alive in the midst of what had become fairly common discounting and bullying. John not infrequently contested the negative stereotyping of Steven.

Steven had been invited to a company Halloween party but had not been told to come in costume. When he walked into the conference room where everyone was gathered, Robert looked puzzled for a moment at the absence of a costume. He then said to Steven, "We'll just say that you came as a Wandering Jew." It was true that Robert had included Steven as "one of us" for the party, but the remark stung. The image of the rootless Wandering Jew, a cursed person without a place or home, had been cast onto Jews for centuries. For the party Robert had cast Steven as a Jew. Steven was beginning to wonder, *Is that who I am to many people?*

Just as Steven came to embody the negative stereotype of the Wandering Jew, if only briefly at the party, he also became the recipient of the idealized and positive stereotype of being one of God's Chosen People, through whom salvation will arrive. As a Jew in the Bible Belt, Steven occasionally received lavish praise, admiration, even adoration for simply being Jewish. He was being magically associated with people's unflinching support for the State of Israel and its policies—and the events that would lead to the Second Coming of Jesus Christ, the Messiah. Many people thanked him for being a Jew—a gratitude whose double-edged sword did not escape him. After all, Jews were expected to bring about Armageddon, and if they did not convert immediately to Christianity, they were condemned to hell. Steven, as either a Wandering Jew or a stand-in for the Second Coming, became a category instead of a person. His identity relative to others' and his colleagues', and even his self-identity, were, it seemed, unavoidably contaminated by the stereotypes associated with being Jewish.

Questions

How common is a story like this in organization(s) where a person (or group) is treated as an Other?

How does this story illustrate some of the challenges of sensitizing employees to the ever-growing diversity in the workplace?

What are the roles of splitting and projective identification in making and sustaining Steven as a target?

How can offhand, seemingly humorous remarks single out and isolate someone?

In what ways is this story an example of widespread, systematic organizational dynamics?

Discussion and Analysis

Episodes like these can, over time, become a heavy burden of stereotypes and projected content. The constant press of stereotypes accumulates, creating aversive self-experience. In this case Steven gradually became known in ways he did not know himself to be, altering his self-experience as well as how others who met him came to know him. He was at times little more than the stereotypes and projections people placed on him. As their Jew, Steven had become a figment of others' imagination and an object in their minds.

Although the story is about an individual member of an organization, it is more widely a story about a modern workplace. It illustrates some common features of the workplace, such as a stranger from a foreign land (the Northeast rather than the Bible Belt) with unconventional knowledge. Steven was clearly a cultural outlier for others, an almost alien presence among the people with whom he worked every day. This potential existed from the outset, and in the story he did become a figment of their imagination. They experienced him at times as a strange and alien presence or object who lost his existence as a separate sentient human being and a subject. By being transformed into an object in their minds, he could be manipulated at will in fantasy. It was also the case that Steven could, because of the constant press of the transference, experience himself as alien to himself. Self-alienation like this often never fully heals and remains a latent potential for regression for those who become overloaded with stereotypes and projections that they cannot stave off, reverse, or shed. The load, in a sense, becomes oppressive as in the case of projective identification, to maintaining one's distinct sense of self.

The experience in the story is all too common at work these days, especially with respect to all the different nationalities, ethnicities, and religions present in the workplace. The story touches upon the larger cultural context, where Steven as a person becomes lost in the workplace, an alien in a foreign land even though he is as American as his colleagues. This story illustrates the unhealthy human tendencies that arise in groups when they encounter a different person, group, or idea (not "us"). Steven's story can also be understood as an out-of-awareness group process aimed at coping with the anxiety of his presence by transforming his alienness into something friendlier, less threatening, more accessible, more positive, and more familiar. They would in a sense control him through projective identification.

The question becomes: Can I or we accept and value Steven for who he is as a separate and distinct human being? Or must we most of the time construct him out of stereotypes and splitting and projection? The story tells a discouraging tale about this prospect in cross-cultural encounter and confrontation—a tale not only about Steven but also about the modern workplace. Despite widespread cultural sensitivity training in the United States, Steven's story remains all too common.

From a psychodynamic perspective the story illustrates how profoundly important it is to appreciate the significance of self-created "self-objects" that are freely manipulated in the mind, mostly out of conscious awareness. *Self-object*, a term coined by Heinz Kohut (1971), refers to an unconscious, almost magically experienced, fusion of one's self-representation with the mental image or representation of another person or group. Equally important is that these states of mind do leak out and influence thoughts, feelings, and actions relative to others. Sometimes people say the oddest things, seemingly out of context. Projection and transference contribute to this situation. Steven's associates invented him in their minds and unwittingly came to know him as conceived by projecting (locating) their fantasized Steven into him (projective identification). These fantasies were what popped out in the story.

Steven in part disappeared as an individual and became a vessel for others' demonizing and idealizing fantasies about the final redemption of the world. Demonization and idealization are the two sides of splitting and projective identification. Steven must be this way or that way.

And this is often accompanied by pathological certainty—there is no doubt that he *is* the way that he is conceived. Once the Steven-as-Other comes into existence, he will most often have attributes that are either loved and admired or feared and hated. These attributes then predictably draw highly energized feelings that are transferred from the past to the present. He may be loved and admired or despised and hated. In these cases the individual becomes the focal point of the mindful manipulations of others, leading to hard-to-fathom interpersonal interactions and outcomes. For Steven they simply fell from the sky on him. Further, Steven also draws or promotes projections onto him simply by being a Jew. Simply by being who he is inadvertently encourages his own victimization, not unlike in the case of sexual harassment.

Yet another important element in this story that should be explored further is the role of projective identification. Projective identification arises when self-content that is undesirable and painful to hold in oneself is split off from self and projected onto others, with the intent of taking them over and controlling them. Steven could easily come to have experienced himself as the Other, consistent with the unconscious fantasies others held toward him, losing parts of himself in the process. Anyone who has the experience of being continually treated and manipulated like an object knows how intensely personal and disruptive a process like this can become. The result can be the emergence of a false sense of self as a result of the unconscious adoption of the projections.

STORY 3
THE TRIAL

Walter, a research scientist in a biomedical organization, had recently lost his trusted and highly effective secretary, who seamlessly managed his life at work. After interviewing several candidates for this half-time secretarial position, Walter chose the candidate who seemed the most self-confident and accomplished. He was soon to regret what ultimately proved to be an irreversible decision. The new secretary would not follow his instructions and did the projects as she deemed fit. When Walter tried to correct her, she would go to his supervisor and complain that *he* was difficult to work with. Invariably, his supervisor, also a female, took the secretary's side, agreeing that Walter was being unreasonable. This escalation and triangulation continued for many weeks.

Walter took the issue to the head of the department, but he refused to get involved and sent him back to his supervisor. Walter felt increasingly trapped by his secretary. On several occasions he did lose control and raised his voice at her out of exasperation.

Walter was eventually summoned to his supervisor's office. He had no idea what this was about. When he entered his supervisor's office, he found five women sitting in chairs. He was ordered to close the office door. In the group were two social scientists (one was Walter's supervisor), a social worker, a research assistant, and Walter's secretary. They proceeded to level their charges against him: he was a bully, an "abusive male," and he would not be allowed to leave the office until he confessed that he was an abusive male who should ask for forgiveness.

Walter was so stunned he did not have the presence of mind and perhaps wherewithal to challenge the group or, if you will, what amounted to a gang assault. They had no right to put him on *trial.* He felt terrified and trapped.

He had no idea how long he was in the room or what words were spoken. It felt like an eternity. Walter remembers hearing repeatedly that he was a bully and an abusive male. The beating was unrelenting. At some point he broke down, sobbing, tearfully confessing that he was an abusive male, and pleading for their forgiveness. He even remembered kneeling before them to ask for forgiveness. Only then did they allow him to leave the office. A few months later the social worker, who was new to the organization, said she didn't quite understand what was happening in the meeting. She said she felt that she had no role to play in it, and she was sorry it was so painful for Walter.

Questions

What are the legal, ethical, organizational, and psychological dimensions of the story?

What were the implicit goals of the group who put Walter on trial and the effects of splitting and projection?

What are the meanings of the group's demand that Walter admit that he is an "abusive male"?

What is the role of humiliation in the story?

What are the psychological dimensions of the *triangle* of Walter, his supervisor, and his secretary?

Discussion and Analysis

Clearly for Walter this was one of the most degrading and humiliating experiences in his life. It became a haunting memory that he did not know what to "do" with, how to resolve, or how to put behind him. Some memories are so vivid that they should not be called mere memories. This was one Walter could not shake off. He could not by force of will relegate it entirely to the past. When he remembers it, he reenters the scene, reliving it and all the associated feelings. In hindsight Walter should have just politely excused himself and walked out or simply suggested this type of issue was the province of Human Resources.

In sharing his story he reported remembering two occasions (there may have been more) in which he lost control out of exasperation and did raise his voice to his secretary. These events were what seem to have led to his being summoned, without warning, to his supervisor's office. Whether this summons was legal or ethical, he did not know. He made no excuses for raising his voice, and he thought he had apologized to the secretary when this happened. But clearly this was not enough for the judge and jury in the room. Walter said he could understand why his female colleagues would be angered by and fearful of his loss of control. At the same time he also felt set upon by the group. He felt he was being treated disrespectfully and that he seemed to have become in their minds an embodiment and personification of bad men and abusive males. He was the male enemy. Outcomes like this contain splitting and projection. On one side is the experience of feeling good and innocent. At the same time the Other is experienced as bad and guilty. There is no question about it. Transference of past thoughts and feelings then arises relative to this in the mental construction of self and other. The Other is not only bad but also despised, hated, and needs to be punished or destroyed as a part of a continuum of life experience where all past injustices and one's experience of them are palpably located in the moment, affecting thoughts, feelings, and actions.

In retrospect, it felt as if the group used the conflict with his secretary as an excuse to humiliate Walter and force him into submission and, in fact, into regression to an almost childlike state. They bullied him and called *him* a bully. There was no question in Walter's mind and heart that he had been wrong to raise his voice to the secretary. The question for him was the right of his supervisor and those present to place him (or anyone) *on trial*. Walter was more than guilty until proved innocent; he was guilty without the possibility of any valid explanation other than that he was an abusive male.

There is room in this story to speak to denial, splitting, and projection fueled by feminist rage. For his accusers, it was Walter who was abusive, whereas the context makes it obvious that it was the reverse. He was being bullied and aggressed. In fact there seems sufficient reason to consider that the secretary was being supported by Walter's boss in opposing Walter's direction and by involving his boss in the first place, who bullied *Walter*. Bullies often have a person higher up in the organization who is their protector and champion. If you push back against the bullying, the bully goes to the higher-ranking person, who is expected to punish the offending target of the bullying. Also, the bully or the superior may well call in others, essentially ganging up to take the target out.

Events like this are often seared in the heart, soul, and memory of the victims. It is hard to move on. Much like sufferers of posttraumatic stress disorder, victims of bullying have a palpable fear that the memory may revisit them without warning, reminding them how very vulnerable they may again become in a moment of time. What should not have happened did in fact happen. In cases like these even after decades it may be hard to accept that it happened. The victim may have a sense of personal failure and engage in self-incrimination for having failed locate a reasonable solution in the moment. This sense of personal failure and self-victimization then plays out in an endless mental loop. In effect, victims punish themselves for not having an effective response in the moment—doing the right thing. This tortured self-victimization produces a much greater punishment than what happened during their trial.

Story 4
Guilty Until Proved Innocent

Tom, the new chair of a large clinical department in a medical school, found he did not have enough time to be chair and still perform research. His grants were running out without renewal. He asked his administrator, Frank, to create a position reporting to him for Tom's highly experienced lab tech, an African American woman in her fifties named Joan. She had followed him across the country to work with him when he accepted the position of chair.

The administrator proposed a job in which Joan's experience could be put to good use. She would provide oversight for the major research enterprise of the department. In particular she would train new lab techs, monitor labs for safe and professional practices, and maintain a huge inventory of scientific equipment scattered in labs on different floors and in different buildings, including a Veterans Administration (VA) hospital.

Joan agreed to take up the new role. Frank initially assigned her the task of developing an accurate inventory of the many millions of dollars' worth of scientific equipment in the department. Some had been improperly disposed of or removed by investigators when they left or had been surplused during the last decade but not removed from the inventory list. The VA hospital had its own list of the equipment located in its facility. This list conflicted with the university's list. Some equipment had missing inventory-control-number stickers. In sum, it was a real mess that required carefully reconciling lists, hunting down and counting equipment, and a familiarity with the many types of equipment and expensive attachments.

After a few months Joan became resistant to receiving supervision from Frank, who eventually asked another direct report, Bill, who was Joan's friend, to supervise her. He did not have any better luck. She eventually came up with a theory that Frank was stealing the lab equipment, but she could not credibly explain to Frank or Bill how she arrived at this theory. In fact her explanation demonstrated that she had little understanding of what she was trying to do in terms of managing the equipment inventory, despite having been coached. After due diligence in trying to train and further supervise her, Bill also gave up and their friendship ended. She was now angry and sure something illegal was going on and that Frank needed to be exposed.

Frank then approached Tom, the chair, to ask him to move Joan back to his supervision or to someone else's supervision. After hearing about the difficulties, Tom's response was to appoint a physician colleague and researcher, Dick, to investigate the situation. Over a number of months Dick slowly interviewed everyone and eventually rendered his opinion that Joan should find work elsewhere. The chair then informed Joan of the findings and said she should look for a new position and that he would keep her on the payroll until she did.

Joan was enraged by this. She contacted a civil rights attorney. The lawyer wrote the president of the university a letter asserting racism. The president and his staff of attorneys instructed the chancellor of the campus, Linda, to investigate. Although Joan did not have a regular faculty appointment, the chancellor decided to use the faculty grievance procedure, which required appointment of a five-person panel of faculty. Two were selected by the chancellor, two were selected by Joan, and the four together selected a fifth as chair. The panel ended up with three energized feminist faculty members who published on the subject of feminism. The two male members were less energized in comparison.

The panel began by summoning Tom, Dick, Frank, and Bill to be interviewed the same day. Each waited his turn in an anteroom. Those who had testified were not allowed to speak to those who were waiting, and discussion between those waiting was also forbidden. The panel eventually hired a consulting company to examine the assertions that equipment had been stolen from inventory.

The response from the consulting group was that the process designed by Frank was outstanding, more thorough than they would have designed. The group found no wrongdoing. This finding left the panel with only the question of racism, to which Joan's attorney had added sexism, and the panel itself added age discrimination. Ultimately, after a few more months of multiple, at times intense and combative, visits by Tom, Dick, Frank, and Bill to testify, the panel issued a report that could be summarized as finding no evidence of theft, racism, sexism, or age discrimination. However, the wording in parts of the report indicated that, despite the lack of proof, the panel still thought that what was alleged to have happened had, in fact, happened.

The chancellor's response was to reject a promotion and pay increase for Frank and assign the director of human resources, Alice, to further research the charges. Joan received a promotion that relocated her to a new role in the university's administration. After several months Alice published a report of her findings based on interviews she said she had conducted. It offered nothing new. However, it turned out she had lied. She had not conducted some of the interviews and in particular had not interviewed Tom as she had claimed. Tom was outraged and brought it to the attention of the chancellor and the president. This eventually led to Alice's termination.

Questions

In this story how did psychological issues complicate what could have been straightforward personnel-reporting-supervision issues?

How did personal relationship issues become group issues?

What roles do splitting and projection play in the unfolding of the story?

Why do you think that the chancellor used a *faculty* grievance process for a nonfaculty employee?

How did a problem with Joan's supervision become a problem of racism and sexism?

Discussion and Analysis

Events like this are not uncommon in large organizations, and they are not the exclusive headache of universities. In this case the charges were not true or accurate. No findings to support them were uncovered. However, the female members of the panel (two of whom were selected by Joan) continually asked questions that at times were aimed at proving what they *believed* had happened. They thought that Tom, Dick, Frank, and Bill were guilty of sexism and racism and had no use for proof to the contrary. However, the absence of proof of wrongdoing did not lead to their exoneration of Joan's allegations. Linda, the chancellor, proceeded to dole out punishment and assigned her HR director to continue to look for evidence.

Eventually Frank concluded that the underlying dynamics were much like sibling rivalry. Consider the following triangle: Frank was now the trusted colleague of Tom, and Joan had lost her favored status with Tom as he lost the grants that paid her salary. Splitting and projection readily explain how someone comes to see another individual as all bad and himself or herself as all good. Frank simply came to be known by Joan and eventually some on the panel as evil. He had to be taken out, although

Frank had extended himself in the first place to try to help her in her new position.

Franco Fornari's felicitous phrase, "the paranoid elaboration of mourning" (1975, p. 219), seems apt here. Rather than accept and grieve her loss of Tom, Joan instead felt Frank had stolen him from her or, in different terms, displaced her from his affection. The same splitting and projection can be said for Bill and eventually Tom himself. This same dynamic was present within the panel researching the charges, where Joan is seen as good and the victim of powerful, younger, white, male managers. This process was sustained for a year, attesting to the power and sustainability of splitting, projection, and accompanying transference that creates an alternate reality resistant to accurate reality testing.

This is also a story about senior executives taking administrative steps to cover themselves in case of a lawsuit and criticism in the media. In particular top management allowed the use of the faculty grievance process for a nonfaculty employee. In many organizations fear, self-interest, and conserving power and reputation often take precedence over reasonable and fair processes.

This story also illustrates how social issues (sexism, racism, age) can be used to inflame individual relational issues and in the process bring a wide array of people and institutions into the conflict. Thus the problematic *personal* relationship between Tom, Joan, and Frank (and others) is translated or reframed as an issue of *group* oppression. Once the problem is defined as emblematic of social issues, the original interpersonal conflict is left behind. Or, to put it another way, the original *interpersonal* conflict is exploited by those who need to see it as an example of intergroup conflict—male versus female, white versus black, old versus young. As so often occurs in organizations, transference replaces reality, generating its own perverse reality that ends up becoming polarized. The two sides fight an ideological battle that in this case started with a need for the chair to abandon his research and honor his commitment to Joan by finding her a position in his department.

Conclusion

The stories in this chapter are about a number of different workplace experiences that provide insight into what leaders as well as all organizational members face. Becoming lost in a constant press of relatively uniform projections based on one's title, ethnicity, religion, gender, or age can become a powerful and transformative experience. One cannot merely be oneself in a role or as a person. Losses of self-integration, one's sense of self, who one is, what one aspires to be—all are at stake in the stories and in all our lives at work as well as outside work. Being aware that this does happen, and understanding the underlying psychodynamics, makes a major contribution to maintaining one's sense of self and, with that, sanity. In providing this awareness and insight we the authors are contributing to a more aware, reflective, insightful, and, we add, sane workplace.

The essential nature and importance of this understanding becomes clear in chapter 6, where the stories describe many hard-to-imagine organizational dynamics. We include some stories about change in which people rise above dysfunctional organizational dynamics to create a better workplace.

CHAPTER 6

Organizational Toxicity

Introduction

Chapters 4 and 5 told stories about and examined leader and leader-follower dynamics, as well as splitting, projection, and transference among employees. The next group of stories focuses on not-so-easily classified organizational dynamics that are equally commonplace. They in part speak to the rather more messy side of trying to understand workplace dynamics that just do not seem to make much sense.

The first three stories speak to altering the perception of reality to meet one's needs or avoiding reality altogether. When life becomes stressful at work, people tend to see and know what they want. The Indian parable of the three blind men and the elephant addresses some of these elements. The parable attests to individual and group dynamics, where an individual or group can believe in the truth of their subjective experience—such as in the parable where the elephant's leg is felt to be a tree, its side felt to be a wall, and its trunk felt to be a snake—but at the same time not appreciate that this experience is inherently limited. It does not account for other subjective truths that may go unknown, uncommunicated, and, if known, not respected. The way one understands reality can be altered by denying some aspects of it, as in selective attention or consciously or unconsciously simply knowing it in a way not consistent with reality. Further, the reality of a situation can be intentionally altered and covered up for business-related reasons.

The next five stories might collectively be described as some of the many faces and forms bad management can take at work. Incentives and the use of temporary employees can, for example, be uncritically relied upon despite information that they do not work and in fact create organizational harm. The stories also address value systems that not only are culturally unacceptable but also introduce serious organizational dysfunctions as well as reality-based fear and paranoia. Some stories also refer to a clear lack of critical thinking informed by accurate reality testing. Why do people continue to do things that do not work? The humorous definition of insanity is doing the same thing over and over and expecting a different outcome. It is worth noting that synonyms for *insanity* are *folly, foolishness, madness, idiocy, stupidity, lunacy,* and *silliness.* These five stories touch upon these synonyms and make it clear that things are not always rational in the workplace.

The next two stories explore a truly darker side of the workplace, when profit and protecting one's ego become the primary considerations for decision making. People and large groups of employees can be terminated without warning, either as a measure of self-vindication or as a larger, more faddish, approach to managing such as organizational downsizing, restructuring, and reengineering.

We conclude with three stories that make it clear that exceptionally dysfunctional workplaces are a choice, an option that seemingly is selected and unquestioningly embraced sometimes for decades. Sometimes the organization or parts of it can be made more functional despite resistance to change. In other cases the organization can begin to be repaired at a more fundamental level only if leaders are willing to take up the challenge to do so.

Story 1
Bad News

The faculty leaders of a large academic department in a university met in a conference room to discuss the results of an external review of their department in anticipation of recruiting a new leader. Everyone had received copies of the review two days earlier so they could read through it; it contained well-founded negative to very negative findings that fairly and accurately portrayed the problems and weaknesses of the department.

The meeting got underway with a dozen faculty leaders from subdisciplines in attendance, along with their interim chair, who led the group. Discussion initially weaved in and out of the numerous negative findings. No one denied the accuracy, but periodically someone would try to add qualifying statements or reasons why the problem arose. A sense of gloom and a lack of energy developed as the meeting progressed. Exposure to all this distressing reality at one time seemed to be overwhelming, hard to comprehend, and depressing. The interim chair eventually suggested using a large whiteboard to develop a synthesized list of the main points of criticism, and those present began to provide a list of bullet points. As the list developed, the group discussed and explored some points, taking up a large part of the meeting. Making the list did not change the group's sense of despair and distress.

One of those present eventually spoke up and said, "We can't be this bad. We have some strengths as well." Everyone present agreed, and the interim chair naturally moved to the other side of the whiteboard to begin making this list. The board was rapidly filled with self-defined strengths, and when the list was about the same length as the list of weaknesses, the hour for the meeting had expired. Everyone present was now feeling much better, and discussions not related to the report broke out as everyone left. The report was later seen on a shelf in the interim chair's office. It was never again discussed in a meeting of these faculty leaders. It was as though it had ceased to exist. Creating the second list of self-generated strengths seemed to have magically annihilated the negative findings in the report. Recruiting for a new chair proceeded without any effort to deal with the negative findings.

Questions

What is the role in the story of departmental leadership in the shift of group focus from discussion of the external review to an enumeration of group strengths?

How can making a work group feel better be a trap that prevents it from accepting and addressing reality?

What was the role of departmental group process in the outcome of the story?

Why do organizational work groups so often fail to deal with reality?

If you had been the interim chair in the story, what might you have done differently?

The leader in the story was the *interim* chair—does that make any difference in the process of the group?

Discussion and Analysis

What was the purpose of the group and the meeting? The story suggests that the answer is neither obvious nor simple. A rational report was essentially annihilated by an unconscious group process that generated another "rational" list of equal length. For every group and meeting there is both the official, conscious, explicit, and perhaps rational agenda— what the group is ostensibly gathered to do—and the unofficial, unconscious, implicit, and perhaps irrational agenda that often conflicts with, if not overrides, the ostensible reason for meeting. Paralleling this is whether the group of people who are gathered actually address reality (the task at hand) or abandon reality and create a world of fantasy.

It seems odd to talk like this about an organizational world that is presumably based on rationality. People want to believe organizations are guided by objective, realistic thinking, planning, and decision making. Yet this story illustrates how groups often deal with receiving bad news, such as a critical external review. Those gathered tried to change feeling bad into feeling good, even if that required abandoning (denying) reality and retreating (regressing) into a shared fantasy world. Group leadership plays a pivotal role in this type of group process.

Consider the group member who said, "We can't be that bad. We have some strengths as well." That can be juxtaposed with the many negative findings listed on the board. At that precise moment the interim chair *could have* identified the wish to feel better and not so depressed. Perhaps he, rather than indulging the group and himself in the wish to feel better by avoiding the reality of the critique, could have added that it was entirely understandable that they felt bad about the report. That is, the leader could have helped the group member—who was probably speaking for the group—to acknowledge and stay with the feelings of sadness rather than flee from them with a manic defense. The chair could have said, for instance, that the faculty would be able to feel good *in the long run* if they improved the department by addressing the criticisms in the report. This would create a better foundation for the department as the professors recruited a new permanent chair. By doing this the interim chair would have returned the group to the task of discussing the external review and determining a course of action to address the criticisms.

In American culture we often speak of how alcoholics deny that they are alcoholics. The story of this faculty meeting shows how groups can also deny reality in order to flee into a fantasy that makes them feel good—for the short run. Instead, the interim chair accepted the unconscious assignment from the group to help members to feel good about the department in the moment by denying the painful substance of the report. He joined them in a denial of reality. He enabled them. This made it unlikely that anything would change for the better before a new chair was appointed. Everything would be dropped into the new leader's lap.

STORY 2

ORGANIZATIONAL COSMETOLOGY

Organizations are bought and sold all the time. Mergers are common. Many of these decisions are based on whether it is less expensive to buy a company that has what you want or to build it yourself. The two options can be roughly compared and their costs calculated by consultants who specialize in this type of decision making.

The Tale of Marketing, Inc.

A telephone marketing organization that sells medical supplies has been exceptionally mismanaged. It was purchased by a larger company, although it had a nearly defunct information system to handle order taking, billing, collections, accounting, shipping, and inventory control. The company that made the software had gone out of business nearly a decade earlier. This required the acquiring company to install a new system that cost more than $5 million. A large consulting company was paid to create the new system customized to the needs of the company. After nearly two years, and well past the due date and substantially over budget, the new system was still not ready to go. The consulting company made this perfectly clear. Nonetheless the CEO mandated the system was to start and the old system was to be turned off, instead running it in parallel for back up.

Almost immediately the new system failed in every aspect of operation. The consulting company was fired, and it sued. The staff responsible for trying to run the system was at a complete loss. Eventually order taking was stabilized and with considerable effort orders were shipped. However billing, collection, and accounting, were not working. Therefore the more that was shipped, the more money the company had to borrow to purchase inventory to ship. After six months of trying to get the new system to work, the parent company decided to sell the company. Salvaging it was simply not possible without investing millions more and suffering more losses.

When the sell decision was made, the divisional CEO went busily about pumping up the sales volume, digging the financial hole deeper and faster in the short run. He was confident the high volume would add to the sale price. The large customer database that had been imported into the new system from the defunct system was, however, found to be seriously compromised and out of date. Large parts of it were of no value at all. A company eventually purchased this failed company to get its customer database because of the sales volume it was generating. The new company had its own computer system and would import the customer database with all its problems into its parent system.

The Tale of TV Station, Inc.

A regional television station was struggling financially and hired a new CEO, Ralph, to turn it around. When he arrived, part of the problem he inherited was that the physical plant and equipment were nearly out of date, and this was generating operating problems. Expensive upgrades were needed. Ralph, however, proved to be resourceful in terms of developing work-arounds to keep the station on the air. Within months the bottom line was looking better. After three years profitability was robust. Ralph was a superstar, and based on this track record he was hired by a major metropolitan station at a much higher salary. After he left, how he did it became clear. Ralph had fired some of the maintenance staff and had stopped buying new equipment and upgrades. His taking a new job was well timed since he knew this strategy of patching things together could not work much longer.

The CEO who replaced Ralph was surprised at how much deferred maintenance and obsolete and nonfunctional equipment the station had. The available cash flow could not nearly accommodate this backlog of needed upgrades. The parent company eventually had to invest millions to keep the station running.

Questions

Does steadfast pursuit of self-interest always or even often produce a common good?

Is it acceptable to manipulate process, data, and reports to optimize one's success at work or convince a buyer that purchasing an organization is a good deal?

How important is due diligence when buying or merging with another organization?

Is it possible to build a career on cutting corners, thereby compromising one's organization?

How ethical is it to put lipstick on the pig? (To "put lipstick on a pig" is a rhetorical expression used here to convey the message that making superficial or cosmetic changes can make a product or organization look better to others while not improving its performance or value.)

Discussion and Analysis

Applying lipstick to organizations to make them look better than they are, such as by temporarily pumping up sales or drastically reducing operating costs to improve the appearance of value, can take many forms. Similarly the lipstick may be applied to make a CEO look good to board members and stockholders. In theory due diligence in examining any purchase or merger should reveal the lipstick. However, many manipulations that achieve these purposes are hard to spot. Further, some organizations acquiring other organizations look right past these efforts. They want only a customer base, distribution system, or locations, as though you can do this without paying attention to the rest of the purchase. Many artificially enhanced CEOs are hired based on nothing more than the performance they *report* they have achieved, including increases in stock value.

The term *caveat emptor*—buyer beware—comes to mind. At least in the United States and its minimally regulated capitalist system, the notion that greed is good often prevails. We might wisely, however, ask *why* senior-level executives act like this, often almost exclusively for their personal benefit and gain. In particular these behaviors might be considered the pathological side of capitalism.

How, then, can these executives ever think that doing the wrong thing is right? Must everyone else assume that they believe what they have done is right? Their rationale is based on a denial of reality (what they are doing is wrong) mixed with a large measure of grandiosity (inflated narcissism). They may so much want to believe their solution is the right one that they believe their own propaganda. They may also, on a darker note, be somewhat psychopathic (Babiak & Hare, 2006; Schouten & Silver, 2012). They may not believe in their myth like snake oil salesmen do, but they nonetheless eagerly persuade others to believe in it. When they do believe it, they are operating without much conscience to set a trap for others to fall into.

In the first story the telemarketing CEO had a need to be right when he wrongly required bringing the new system online. When operations blew up, he sacrificed the consulting company that was developing the system, even though its people had told him the truth. What George Devereux long ago called the "vicious cycle of psychopathology" (1956) ensued. More and more attempts were made to shore up and salvage the inherently flawed system, eventually leading to the sale of the company, which was artificially made to look better than it was. Likewise, in the second story, CEO Ralph also turned out to be an organizational illusionist, making decisions that served only his interests, self-promotion and career advancement. The way he "turned around" the TV station was to lay employees off and indefinitely postpone maintenance of and upgrades to the physical plant, making an already bad problem worse. He was slowly gutting the organization, not unlike many CEOs since the early 1980s who have pursued popular management fads like downsizing and venture capitalists who carve up companies, sell off the pieces, and raid retirement funds.

In these cases the predatory psychology of the leader meets the group psychology of boards of directors, trustees, and shareholders, who sometimes seek profit at any cost. The charisma of the leader is matched by the group members' wish to believe. They are in essence made for each other. They are willing to embrace a shared delusion enabled by rationalization, denial, and selective attention. They all become convinced that they have done nothing much to gussy up the pig. In the final analysis making it pretty is expected and not particularly unethical. It is the way of capitalism. The buyer must beware. This way of doing business is underscored by the investment bankers who sold toxic assets to buyers who could not understand what they were purchasing. The bankers assured the buyers these were sound investments, and of course the investments were highly rated by Standard & Poor's, Moody's, and Fitch. How could anything go wrong?

Story 3
Why Didn't They Ask?

The chair and administrator of the OB/GYN department in a large medical school thought they had billing problems related to the health care that one of their specialty divisions was providing. The new division chief, who had worked in private practice, thought there was a problem. Medicine, another large department, which had a small staff of experienced analysts and billing experts, was asked to volunteer to help solve these problems. This was done over a few weeks. Major issues were found, recommendations provided, and changes implemented. Billing for the OB/GYN division substantially improved, as did documentation in its medical charts. During their work for OB/GYN the staff from Medicine noticed a variety of equally bad problems in other OB/GYN divisions that were costing the department hundreds of thousands of dollars in lost income.

During the final meeting with the OB/GYN chair and his longtime administrator, the Medicine staff pointed out that further improvements could be made in other divisions and that Medicine staff members would provide additional free consultation if the chair would like them to do so. The chair looked at his administrator and asked her if she was aware of any other problems, to which she responded no. The chair then respect-

fully declined the offer without asking why Medicine had made the suggestion. Medicine staffers did not push the point because they were, after
all, volunteering more free effort. Given the considerable expertise of the
Medicine staff and the success of the consultation and intervention, one
might think the OB/GYN chair might have asked more questions about
the proposed free consultation. Why didn't he?

Questions

Why would the chair and his administrator forgo the opportunity
to increase billing and therefore profitability?

What factors could lead the chair and his administrator to fail to
accept reality?

What do you think Medicine's billing staff felt when the chair declined the offer of further improvement?

What might be the role of narcissism in this story?

How common are events like this in the workplace?

Discussion and Analysis

Unconscious collusion between the chair and the administrator might
account for the lack of inquiry. Collusion like this often arises between
two individuals as a result of their long relationship with each other.
Each learns to be protective of the other. Learning about additional problems would have been potentially distressing to both. From the chair's
perspective, prying the lid off a Pandora's box of unknown proportions
could be threatening in terms of exposing financial problems that would
reflect poorly upon his leadership and his administrator's performance.
Implicit within this is exposing such elements as the chair's ignorance of
professional fee billing and fear of having to deal with colleagues in regard to their poor administration of their divisions—conflict avoidance.
Fear of shame or embarrassment is an important concern for physician
executives. What kind of leader would let all this financial irresponsi-
bility happen? In the choice between forthrightly addressing reality and
protecting the chair's self and public images as well as his administrator's
reputation, the chair chose the second course. Put another way, protect-

ing the fragile self of the chair (protection from narcissistic injury) and avoiding stressful interpersonal conflict was more important than putting the department on sounder financial footing. Also neither the chair nor the administrator may have pursued this review if not for the pressure applied by the new division chief, who understood billing from his experience in private practice.

The administrator might then reasonably want to protect her boss for the reasons that they consciously and unconsciously share. However, she might also be fearful of being exposed for allowing a large amount of financial waste, because her job description included financial management and oversight of professional fee billing. Self-preservation is a strong motivator.

That other divisions in the department were failing to bill for hundreds of thousands of dollars in professional fees leads to consideration of a wider set of collusive dynamics involving faculty, division chiefs, and their administrators. How could so many people who could benefit from improved department finances be so unaware of, or indifferent to, the possibilities? Such resistance to knowing this had to be a well-established, shared social defense. Mutual face saving and the protection of fragile selves had become a higher priority than generating hundreds of thousands of dollars in revenue.

From an administrative perspective it would be fair to ask, "How stupid could they be?" Not to be ruled out is that the chair and his administrator simply were ignorant (unknowing) of the many elements that created these missed billing opportunities. The department was doing well enough financially, and they had little financial pressure to learn and earn more. This indifference and self-imposed ignorance, defended by simply not paying attention (selective attention), could explain it. They did not ask the billing experts why they offered more free consultation because there was no perceived need—no awareness. Not everyone in the workplace is bright, informed, striving for excellence, and open to change. Also they may well have pursued this consultation only to placate the new division chief. With the free work done and the improvements implemented, the task was completed and the division chief was assuaged. Perhaps even more interesting is that the new division chief apparently did not bring to the attention of other division chiefs the billing problems that might well exist in their divisions. Self-interest in this case wins out.

This story ends with the irrationality of losing hundreds of thousands of dollars in revenue from services already rendered but not properly billed. The potential explanations—psychological defensiveness, shared group defenses, and ignorance—answer the question "Why didn't they ask?" and the further, haunting question "What would they *lose* if they asked?"

STORY 4
WELLNESS CENTER NOT SO WELL MANAGED

Rob was working as a consultant for an organization that developed a wellness resource center. The center used nurses to speak with employees of contracted companies about health problems and to follow those with chronic conditions. Elmer, the vice president over these areas, eventually asked Rob to help solve operating problems in the wellness resource center.

The center had about seventy-five registered nurses seated at nice workstations equipped with computer screens and a sophisticated phone system that could be centrally monitored. The center was just getting started and was now preoccupied with enrolling employees of a large international company. The new contract made participation optional so it was critically important to proactively enroll as many employees as possible to optimize income from the contract.

Enrollment, however, was lagging. A full-time staff of fifteen employees had been tasked with making the first contact and enrolling the employees, who would then be contacted by the nurses to further introduce the program and gather health information to be entered into newly designed in-house software. The process seemed straightforward but was not performing well.

An inspection of the work of the fifteen staff revealed that the data base they were using did not allow them to easily track how many times someone had tried to contact an employee. Ascertaining this took several minutes and required opening a number of screens. The system flagged those who were enrolled, but they remained in the call list, which could not be sorted to yield only those employees who were not enrolled. In fact finding someone to call was taking much more time than making the call. The effort was slowly grinding to a halt. This was made painfully clear after Thomas, the manager of enrollment, was asked to time how many outgoing calls were being made an hour and how long it took to locate someone to call.

Thomas presented these findings at a meeting but also defended his staff by asserting they were achieving outstanding performance given the limitations. Rob asked Thomas to provide data to prove the outstanding performance. A week later Thomas reported that five of the fifteen employees had turned out to be poor performers, and he had terminated them. During the meeting Rob recommended the nurses adopt a paper-and-pencil system that would keep track of those enrolled and when calls had been placed. While seemingly a step backward from computing, this manual system was effective, and enrollment figures began to improve.

During this several-week interval the CEO, Paul, demanded to know why enrollment performance had lagged. Elmer turned to Rob to generate a detailed report, which Rob did in collaboration with Thomas, thereby promoting ownership on Thomas's part. Rob blended the timed studies into a five-page report that detailed the many failings of the software to support enrollment activity, especially its inadequate support for the nurses making the wellness calls. The nurses were wrestling with an overengineered design for the clinical database that was not user friendly and slowed their work significantly. They were in fact working around the system to do their job.

A meeting was scheduled with the chief information officer, Sam. Sam was a close friend of Paul, the CEO of the company. Sam had spearheaded the design and development of all the software used by the wellness center. It was his baby. Present were Elmer, Thomas, and Sam, plus several staff members brought by Thomas and Sam. The report was handed out, and everyone had a few minutes to read it. Sam, the CIO, showed visible signs of discomfort as he read it. When everyone was finished reading, discussion began. Sam dominated the discussion, making several suggestions to change wording and delete content. When taken together, his suggestions gutted the report. Thomas and his staff began to show signs of distress as Sam mentioned one change after another. Elmer seemed ready to go along rather than confront Sam, whom he knew would take any such move directly to Paul, who was apt to be confrontational.

Rob, the expendable consultant, eventually stated the obvious: "If you make these changes, the report will not answer the CEO's question." Sam then declared the report was unacceptable and that he would prepare his own report for Paul, the CEO. Thomas returned to his staff, focusing thereafter on improving the manual enrollment system that ironically had to be concealed from Sam and Paul when they walked through the area. The nurses continued to figure out how to work around the limitations of the clinical database.

Questions

How important is it to use data-driven analyses in evaluating employee and system performance?

In preparing a detailed description of an operating problem, how important is it to protect those who designed and operated the business process from feeling threatened?

How important is it to know the network of personal friends as well as enemies among managers and executives before pointing out an operating problem?

Is it important to speak of and write about operating problems in a way that does not embarrass those involved in creating the problem?

How important is it to have clear and well-developed performance standards for employees that are discussed with employees on a regular basis?

Discussion and Analysis

When an organization is toxic, it is often toxic throughout, which tends to result from a leader who infects the organization with the leader's pathology through selective hiring and retention. It is not uncommon to find chief executives who have gathered around them a group that, in return for its loyalty, enablement, and provision of narcissistic supplies for the leader, receives special status relative to everyone else. Members of this group are promoted more often and receive higher salaries. They may also frequently socialize with the leader outside work. As a result an organizational split with accompanying projections develops. There are those who have special status and those who do not.

Anyone calling into question what one of these special people is doing may well be seen as bad and a threat and therefore may be attacked by one or more of the special status people. However, if the special people do not succeed in neutralizing or eliminating the offending individual themselves, they may recruit the CEO to support them, perhaps by resorting to using false or distorted information about the person to get the CEO to act.

Employees' general knowledge of these events promotes fear and anxiety that they will be targeted. Paranoia and interpersonal defensiveness become the undiscussable norm. Trust and respect are largely absent. Speaking up is career threatening. Surviving in a workplace like this is a testament to human plasticity and adaptability. In some ways the response may be described as a shared social defense. Employees learn from each other what works and what does not, as evidenced by those who have been terminated. This shared response can become so pervasive that describing it as part of the organizational culture can be appropriate.

In organizations where there is this much potential danger to personal survival, employees learn to keep a low profile, blend in, and try not to be singled out as different. They often isolate themselves in their workstations, offices, or cubicles—in the belief that not being seen means that they won't be singled out. A persecutory atmosphere like this can hang like a thick pall over a workplace. Anxiety and fear are readily evoked. Such an atmosphere provokes persecutory transference on the part of almost everyone, since no one ever knows who will be next. People fear to speak up lest they offend the special people.

In this story Sam's "baby" (and the CEO's collusion) merits a final mention. In many workplaces executives have babies of this sort, which can be ideas, mission statements, visions, and special projects that no one dares to criticize. Discussion of these babies becomes an organizational taboo consistent with someone who is untouchable in the sense of high status and power. An almost religious, or sacred, aura can develop around the idea or project and the person. This outcome is fueled by idealization. Projective identification is usually associated with getting rid of some unacceptable, demonized part of oneself and forcing it into another person or group, which takes it in and becomes like the projections. The opposite is the idealization of certain people, ideas, or things that are beyond reproach. In this case what are gotten rid of and located in the other through projections are one's good qualities such as creativity, innovation, vision, and ability to act decisively to implement change. The other people or group accepts these projections and comes to know themselves or the group as having these good qualities.

STORY 5

THE TEMPS

A new turnaround CEO with a background in marketing set to work to improve a large independent clinical laboratory in a major city. He was effective at marketing and selling, and he quickly managed to acquire several major contracts with large local companies. These contracts led to thousands of employees who had questions about the new program, its costs, and how it worked. Since the CEO had focused his attention on getting the contracts, he had given little thought to the staffing implications of obtaining the contracts.

Incoming calls immediately overwhelmed the staff. They had been effectively supporting a few small contracts. The CEO's response was to contract with a temp agency to provide employees to staff the phones and handle often challenging and complex questions from patients. The twenty or so temps showed up within a few days. They had no training or previous experience. The few trained and experienced employees had to be taken off the phones to train and supervise the temps. Some temps learned quickly and became fairly effective. However, some performed poorly, and others were undependable and did not consistently show up to work.

As the calls poured in, the supervisors made their best effort to train and supervise the temps. However, this work was made much more difficult because the temps stayed only a few weeks or months and were moved to other jobs by the temp agency. After all, they were temps and not permanent employees. This continuous turnover undermined the ability to train them to meaningfully answer patient questions, because each new temp had to learn the job anew.

After a few months of this the CEO understood he had to hire full-time employees. He had been avoiding doing this because of the expense. The temps and their marginal productivity were less expensive than recruiting and hiring qualified people. At this point the poor customer support for the contracts began to attract negative attention from the two large employers. They began to threaten to pull their contracts. The fear of losing the contracts brought the hiring process to a halt before full-time employees were hired. The temps would have to do. This created a self-fulfilling prophecy, and the contracts were ultimately lost.

Temps had also been hired to staff other areas in the lab, as were a number of independent consultants to improve various operating areas. One area that had been staffed by temps dealt with the receipt of checks from various organizations and patients paying for services rendered. Eventually this area went unstaffed altogether. One day a consultant who had been hired to look at the incoming call service and its problems sat at a desk in this area and looked through one of many hundreds of envelope-size boxes. He opened a few envelopes. Each held a check. A review of fifty more revealed that almost all had checks in them. This was revenue this cash-strapped lab needed.

Because they had not been trained to handle these checks, the temps had dutifully placed all the envelopes in the boxes. Apparently processing them for deposit was not part of what the temps had been trained to do. An estimate based on the average value of the fifty envelopes multiplied by the number of envelopes per box and multiplied by the number of boxes revealed hundreds of thousands of dollars in payments that had never been processed. An employee with the requisite experience was located, and the consultant coached the manager of the area to allow the employee to take the time to make the deposits.

Questions

How is this story one about the CEO's inability to anticipate consequences of his decision making?

How does this story illustrate the limits of the widely accepted rational "economic man" model? (Economic man is a hypothetical individual who acts logically, based on good information but also entirely out of self-interest).

In what ways did the consultant's approach to problem solving differ from the CEO's?

What are some of the consequences of the CEO's priorities for the employees' morale, productivity, and anxiety?

How does this story illustrate the characteristics of narcissistic leadership?

Discussion and Analysis

Blind faith in the rational and predictable economic actor, or economic man model, of decision making by CEOs and management of for-profit businesses is often not supported by reality. This independent lab had been run into the ground by its previous top management as well as to some extent by the new CEO. It was ultimately financially and operationally unsalvageable. The fallback strategy was to sell it to a large national company.

This CEO hired not only temps but also a cadre of consultants to try to patch up the operations. Some had success repairing major problems in the areas assigned to them, while others did not. This ultimately undermined operations, even though some areas were running better. Add to this a willingness of this CEO, who had only marketing experience, to try to manage operations that he had no experience with, and no apparent native talent for, and you have a formula for failure.

The consultant engaged to help with the call center and who also worked on other projects was seen as effective, and the staff often turned to him for management decisions. Occasionally someone would articulate the wish that the consultant remove the CEO, who staffers saw as erratic, lacking important skill sets, and in general making a mess of the company that they depended on for their livelihood. People who had been there for years were beginning to sense that systemic failure was leading to bankruptcy or sale.

Employees were angry and fearful of losing their jobs and even of not getting paid. Cash flow was not dependably sufficient to consistently make payroll. In many areas the employees were keeping the organization running despite being undermined by the CEO's misguided efforts to manage operations. Although the consultant had to respectfully decline to make major decisions or embrace the fantasies of removing the CEO, the staff continued to ask for consultation on a daily basis.

The consultant began to focus on empowering the staff by developing management information and educating them about basic management methods that permitted them to do their work better and solve problems. Thus she gradually returned to the employees their projections onto her of being the one person who was effective. She initially served as a container for the chaos by listening, conducting analyses, and providing clear direction and training. Doing so drew positive and idealizing projections to her initially. However, as the initial chaotic situation became less distressing, she worked with individuals and groups to help them gain more control of their work, systems, and processes. They and the consultant became more effective.

The CEO proved to be more interested in himself and his income than anything else. He enjoyed holding court over dinner, where he took great pleasure in talking about himself. He most often dismissed efforts to discuss operating problems or other topics. At some level he understood that he did not know how to run the business, as evidenced by the hiring of the cadre of consultants. Doing so was better than trying to do it himself. However, he did not always hire the right consultants for the job, and he did not step back sufficiently to appreciate that hiring consultants and temps was not working.

It eventually became apparent that he was working on selling the company for the venture capitalists who owned it. It would not be too speculative to assume that he was trying to hold the operation together only long enough to sell it. If the early goal was turning it around, it apparently had been abandoned. Hiring all the temps and consultants made some sense if his immediate goal was selling the company. However, it was clearly a failed strategy for managing it as an ongoing organization, which perhaps quickly led to the need to sell the company. Dynamics like this are often attributable to overly self-confident, narcissistically driven CEOs. They do not mind being manipulative, concealing their real motives, and using people and organizations to become wealthy.

Finally, the common practice of hiring temporary employees instead of full-time employees should be explored. Executives at organizations from corporations to universities have come to prefer short-term employees and having few reciprocal obligations to them (such as benefits). Universities, for example, now teem with adjunct professors who are hired for one semester to teach a class. They receive a paycheck and that is all, no benefits. Corporations similarly prefer temporary employees for a narrowly defined role, function, or project. Management's wish and assumption is that using temps will lower costs without adversely affecting performance.

This story strongly suggests the opposite. Use of temps to staff an organization is often inefficient and expensive in the long run. To the detriment of customer-organization relationships, employees rarely stay around long enough to become familiar with the full range of the role in which they are placed. An official job description rarely encompasses all that a person does. Psychologically this hiring strategy suggests that narcissism has free rein. There is no commitment to a long-term relationship. Harry Levinson (1962) described a willingness to enter into a long-term workplace relationship as a "psychological contract" between employer and employee. This was commonly the case from the 1930s to the 1980s. Regrettably people have been turned into "human resources" to be allocated and manipulated to meet the needs of the moment. As a result a person in a position becomes a function or a set of functions—a thing. Lost is the sense of membership in a valued group and the network of informal relationships that makes an organization work. Also lost are the emotionally fulfilling aspects of work life that add important value beyond the paycheck. The "temping" of the United States may, then, be examined for its potentially destructive effect on the workplace, organization, and organizational performance.

Story 6
The Flaw

The new CEO of a division composed of several organizations, one of which was a telephone marketing unit for diabetes supplies, inspected the sales trend of this unit and found it to be wanting. In particular he promised the president of the company that he would meet aggressive sales targets to earn extra compensation. The unit was composed of 150 telephone marketers and a small group of managers and supervisors. Toward the end of a month, when sales to date were lower than his forecast, the CEO intervened by offering the telephone marketers a monetary incentive to meet the forecast. The staffers, who included people with high school diplomas and retired executives with multiple degrees who were earning extra income, figured out how to meet the target and thereby earn the incentive.

The rational response by the employees was to call people they regularly serviced and sell them diabetes supplies in advance of need. This immediately increased sales so that they could meet their sales quota and earn the incentive. They then delayed shipping the supplies for a month to meet insurance criteria about billing. During the last week of the month sales increased but only to the level indicated by the CEO as the cut-off for earning the incentive. After all, the employees did not want to create too many advance orders to avoid having fewer orders to take during the next month. Everyone was pleased with the higher sales volume, disregarding for the time being the delayed shipping. The CEO made his numbers for the month and received his bonus.

The next month the employees anticipated that the CEO would once again offer an incentive if their sales lagged. They delayed making calls until the last week, when the CEO responded with the predicted new incentive. This time, having set aside a robust call list for sales calls that should have been made earlier in the month, the staff easily generated a big increase in sales for the last week. However, they also had to borrow sales from the next month as well since the CEO had raised the bar for receiving the bonus. And so it went for a number of months. The CEO made his sales numbers, received his bonus, and felt like an effective executive by providing incentives to manipulate employee performance.

Eventually the telephone marketers had borrowed sales from the future to the maximum extent possible. Not making the sales numbers was inevitable. There would be a month with a serious shortfall in sales. However, they continued to bank easy sales for the end of the month to motivate the CEO to give them more rewards.

Questions

What unanticipated consequences made the incentives approach disastrous?

How was the president of the company complicit in the eventual shortfall in sales?

In what way was the incentive system a failure for both CEO and staff?

What is the belief system or ideology that underlies financial incentives?

What alternatives to incentives might increase sales?

Discussion and Analysis

This story demonstrates the flaw in thinking that one can easily and successfully use incentives to achieve meaningful outcomes for an organization. Implicit in this story is the use of incentives to manipulate human behavior. The underlying assumption is that people will rationally change their behavior to receive the reward, not unlike a dog that sits to receive a treat. The employee sees sufficient benefit in receiving the reward to work harder. This rational decision maker is often described as the economic man.

Incentives are a form of behavior modification. Most often they are discussed as positive extrinsic reinforcement such as a monetary reward for greater performance. Extrinsic incentives can be compared to intrinsic motivation where employees are self-motivated and strive to fulfill personal goals or an organizational ideal to achieve excellence in their work. Few advocate the threat of punishment, which is also a form of incentive implicitly, if not actually, commonly present in the workplace.

However, to the observer of behavior in the workplace, finding substantial unintended consequences as the result of executives' offering incentives is all too common. A proponent of the economic man model and the use of incentives might assert that when incentives produce negative unintended consequences, the incentives are misaligned or poorly managed or the executives did not use information available to monitor productivity. Presumably the problem is then not the use of incentives but how they are designed and administered. A response like the one in

the story, however, largely denies that manipulating employees is expo-
nentially more complex than managing and supervising them without
the use of incentives.

The story underscores that incentive structures are notoriously tricky
to create and manage. Human beings are smart and creative. This means
that the people offering incentives are often unable to predict all the ways
that people will respond to them. Nonetheless executives and managers
still offer them. This calls into question *their* motivations and even the
rationality of doing so. Offering incentives may be viewed as irrational
faith in a process that is known to create unintended consequences, as in
the story.

The tenacity of managers' and organizational leaders' faith in incentives exemplifies a widespread human affliction: the inability to learn
from experience (Bion, 1962). Consider a well-known parallel. The practice of endlessly "tweaking" (slightly modifying) the incentive is akin to
ancient Greek and Roman astronomers constantly "tweaking" the Ptole-
maic earth-centered model of the universe with ever smaller "cycles" and
"epicycles" of planets' and stars' movement (based on the treatise *Almag-
est* by Greco-Egyptian Claudius Ptolemy of Alexandria). They couldn't
get it right because they were *using the wrong mode*—one that they insisted was infallible. Only when Copernicus and Galileo came along and
placed the sun at the center of the solar system did the need for all the
earlier, endless adjustments come to an end. But even then the Catholic
Church nearly executed Galileo because of the dogma that the earth was
the center of the universe.

The model for economic incentives theory is based on an ideology that
its true believers hold to be absolute, incontestable truth. Psychodynamically, reliance on incentives has a delusional quality. The ideology replaces
reality and becomes reality. Doubting the ideology is out of the question
since it is the way. Anyone who expresses doubts may be seen as an un-
informed and/or a poorly performing executive or employee, leaving the
individual open to punishment, rejection for calling into question what
everyone else is doing, and perhaps even termination to eliminate the
critical thinker. The ultimate purpose of an ideology is to diminish the
anxiety that complexity arouses. To learn from experience, effective and
insightful leaders and managers must be able and willing to accurately
test reality. In the story the employees and CEO would have had to con-

sider the unintended consequences of their economic man model, which they presumed was rational, and reconsider the model in the light of the new data—the actual response to the incentives.

STORY 7
KNOWING THE COST OF EVERYTHING
AND THE VALUE OF NOTHING

A consultant is working on performance problems for a telephone marketing company, when an unexpected problem is uncovered. During the past year the company had hired a top-flight marketing executive to develop an advertising program linked to an 800 number. When the marketing strategy and advertising program rolled out nationally, it quickly proved to be a success. The program had been provided a budget by the chief financial officer (CFO) for development, advertising costs, and a staff of twenty telephone marketers. The success of the initial roll-out began to keep the twenty staffers busy. Recently, as the advertising continued, the volume of incoming calls exceeded the ability to answer them. The automated system asked callers to leave a message and their number for a callback (outgoing call).

Calling back began to be a problem. The staff members were burdened most of the time with answering the incoming calls, and the inability to answer all the calls all the time continued to add to the callback list, which had grown to thousands. The manager requested additional staffers so that the program could make more sales. The CFO rejected the request. The explanation was that it was not in the budget. The CFO, however, had learned about the lengthy return call list and ordered the staff to focus on the callbacks, thereby reducing the time available to answer new incoming calls.

This change in method was quickly found to be a mistake. The telephone marketers closed only 40 percent of the outgoing calls, compared with nearly 80 percent of the incoming calls, since the incoming calls were from people ready to sign up. With the same staffing and a 40 percent closure rate, sales began to fall. Eventually sales were below target, and predictably the CFO recommended the marketing program be canceled for low productivity.

Many of the telephone marketers, the marketing executive who designed the program, and the senior management at the site took pleasure in telling the consultant the story. They considered top management and the CFO to be a bad joke. They could not believe what had happened. They could only laugh it off.

Questions

What was the process by which the initial success of the telephone marketing program was turned into failure?

What psychodynamic that accompanies envy and arrogance might explain the CFO's decisions?

What is the role of humor in helping people at many corporate levels adapt to, and make sense of, the CFO's irrational behavior?

What made the experience painful to the telephone marketers and others?

When corporate leaders' decision making defies logic, how can one figure out the psychological explanations that might apply?

Discussion and Analysis

The myth that for-profit corporations are rational and systematically exploit income-generating opportunities is undermined by a story like this. The CFO sabotaged a successful marketing program generating high income. The program was then closed instead of correcting the problem by increasing the budget to capture more sales. How could this happen? In particular events like this demonstrate how difficult effective upward communication is in organizations. And in this story in particular, no one was willing to defy the powerful CFO by going around him to the CEO.

As the story demonstrates, nonsensical decisions by top management are often greeted with disbelief, derision, and humor by those who must suffer the ramifications of the decisions. In this case the painful experience was told to the consultant with humor. Each step in the process was carefully revealed and explained for its humor. They had succeeded but were undermined and ultimately failed. Seemingly all they could do was laugh it off as a part of mourning their loss.

The story also underscores how dangerous it is to cross powerful senior executives who may well respond vindictively by firing those who dare to defy them. Unilateral power like this exists only in some settings, such as a corporate hierarchy. It was clear to those who told the story that they would have been fired in a minute had they decided to do anything about the situation.

The story also makes clear that doing things strictly by the numbers, which at times masquerades as rational decision making, sometimes accomplishes just the opposite. In this story, since the original budget did not accommodate the success of the program, no more staff could be hired despite the apparent profitability of the program. The CFO knew the *cost* of the program but not its *value* to the organization.

A story like this also shows that decision making that defies logic can demoralize a large staff of people, stifling creativity and a willingness to extend themselves in their jobs to achieve outstanding work. Why bother? Those who told the story were using humor to say they were alienated and that they had stopped trying to improve sales.

If this story defies logic, what psycho-logic, so to speak, might help us understand the CFO's decision making? Was he unconsciously self-destructive? His fatal flaw was that he was unable to revise his initial financial plan and budget. Perhaps he feared looking bad to others and the CEO if he changed his mind. Perhaps he thought so highly of himself (excessive narcissism) that he thought he couldn't be wrong. Or perhaps he was aware of the much larger callback list and thought it should be reduced so that he appeared to be in control of the program and its operation. Another possibility is that he gained sadistic pleasure in punishing the group and its leaders for a previous narcissistic injury to him. Or perhaps the substantial success of the program made him look bad in some way that required vindicating his arrogant pride. For example, he might have argued against developing the program, saying that it would never work or that it cost too much to try. At the very least he was clearly unable to learn from experience (Bion, 1962). By limiting his thinking, he made the telemarketing company lose many potential customers and sales.

Splitting, projection, and transference were also likely at work in the story. If the managers in charge of the program had offended the CFO while setting up the program or as a result of their success, the CFO might easily see the managers, staff, and program as bad and as wanting to spend more money than budgeted. He might very well see himself as protecting the organization from these managers and their out-of-control spending. If so, he had to contain them, cut them down to size, and cast them as incompetent to discredit them. Conversely it was easy for the managers and staff to peg the CFO as incompetent and even evil, in the sense that he was harming them and their work and undermining their successful marketing and sales program.

More broadly why was the CFO allowed to get away with such poor planning, that is, why did other senior managers fail to talk with him and urge him to revise his decisions? Losing one's job is never a good option, and his colleagues, whom he could not terminate, faced the likelihood of being added to his payback list. Also to be considered are unwritten rules, such as never questioning anyone's authority and decision making. Yet another possible, if not likely, scenario is that other senior managers were thinking and working in their own closed organizational silos and could not think about anything that was happening "outside the silos." Making sure a good program was maintained outside for those in another silo was not their job, responsibility, or concern. Last, the role of the CEO needs to be considered. The CFO might have played an unconscious role for the CEO, that is, the CEO may have used the CFO as an instrument of control and discipline. Perhaps having a CFO who behaved badly and was seen by others as a bad joke made the CEO look better in comparison—more friendly and supportive and a better leader. A dynamic like this would be fueled by splitting and projection, where the CEO locates in the CFO denied aspects of himself, such as suspicion, high control, and a willingness to punish others for perceived offenses.

We are left to marvel at how irrational many workplaces are. It seems inconceivable that a company would end a successful program, but then again poor management decision making can often undermine programs, the people who staff them, and those who are trying to make them work. They simply have to grin and bear it.

Story 8
Look Up

In 1970 the war in Vietnam was still grinding on for the modern navy, whose fleet relied in part on warships that served in World War II. Such was the case for the World War II destroyers stationed at a naval station in Florida. A Gearing-class destroyer returning from deployment to Vietnam was added to a destroyer stack, which is a group of destroyers tied up side by side. Normally, the entire stack is pulled out from the pier, allowing the returning destroyer to be tied up in the innermost position next to the pier; in this way the outermost destroyer is ready for deployment. However, in this case, when the stack was pulled out, the destroyer already tied up to the pier remained tied up.

This particular destroyer, it turned out, was slated to be towed to a nearby facility to be scrapped. Soon after arriving in Florida, the sailors from the returned destroyer were asked to inspect it for parts that could be cannibalized. (Parts for these old destroyers were scarce.) A tour of the ship revealed just about everything had already been removed. It was largely an empty shell.

After a few weeks a large floating crane came alongside the destroyers to lift heavy equipment and pallets of supplies onto them. This proved to be true for even the about-to-be-scrapped destroyer. In fact several pallets of five-gallon cans of paint were neatly deposited on the bow, and the crew immediately began the chore of storing them. An observer might have wanted to know why a destroyer about to be cut up for scrap metal was being painted, and, even more to the point, why did it still have a fairly large crew?

The question was put to an old chief petty officer. He looked up and pointed to the sky. "See that long flag? It is a commissioning pennant." It turned out the presence of the pennant meant the ship was still commissioned, even though it was an empty shell. "Okay, but why were they painting it?" The chief said that approximately one-third of the crew had to always be present on a commissioned ship to get the ship under way in case of an emergency.

The chief went on to anticipate the next question and answer it. The navy regulation about keeping a third of the crew on the ship at all times was a response to Pearl Harbor. Many ships that were sunk or damaged during the attack were not able to get under way (their best defense for an air attack) or to fire their guns because most of the crews were on liberty. And there you have the rest of the story.

Questions

Why was the destroyer that would soon be made into scrap metal being painted?

Might there be some advantages to keeping an inoperable ship on a list of commissioned ships?

What are the roles of symbolism and ritual in this story?

How would you speculate the one-third of the crew who had to occupy the empty shell felt about painting the ship?

What role did the experience of time and its passage play in this story?

What is the role of irrational thinking in this story?

Discussion and Analysis

In the classic musical *Fiddler on the Roof*, Tevyeh, the poor Jewish milkman, thunders, "Tradition!" when beset by the frightening change happening all around him. People in families, communities, religions, ethnic groups, corporations, and nations all invoke tradition to stop or prevent something from happening. The purpose of insisting on tradition is to freeze time. "We have *always* done it this way" is a common refrain. Often what happens at work makes no logical sense in the present, although people defend it for multiple and often irrational reasons. If a tradition is not responsive or adaptive to current reality, what accounts for its hold on people?

This hold is often why organizational ossification develops and locks in tradition, blocking change. People and groups often stick with what is familiar, resisting all kinds of organizational change. Power and authority held by a few may make it dangerous to call tradition into question. They may oppose change because it threatens their power, control, status, and position. It may also expose them to new challenges they wish to avoid or even expose them as poor managers for not changing on a timely basis. Also to be considered is fear of one's own aggression and rebellion against leaders who want change that will *replace* the tradition—"how we do things here."

Enter now the story. Why was there unquestioning adherence to situationally specific and dysfunctional naval policies and customs? Put a different way: In what framework would these nearly thirty-year-old policies and customs make sense? It is not enough to dismiss the practices as crazy. It turns out a widely shared unconscious story is behind these practices. In a situation in which no danger is imminent, why do people act as if danger could occur at any time and by complete surprise?

The answer lies in the way time is experienced. Apparently the Japanese air attack on the U.S. Navy at Pearl Harbor on December 7, 1941, was at once a historic event and an imminent possibility. The trauma of

Pearl Harbor could not yet be put entirely in the past and left there. Every year the attack is ritually and consciously remembered on its anniversary. It is a haunting presence to the U.S. Navy everywhere and anywhere, forever perhaps. Pearl Harbor was an unfinished mass trauma that still haunted thirty years later. The commissioning pennant linked Florida in 1970 to Pearl Harbor, Hawaii, in 1941. Somewhere in the naval mind, the two were merged.

The danger was generalized, universalized, and in the process removed from both specific time and place. This is why in this story a gutted but still-commissioned destroyer had to have a third of its crew on board; to stay busy the crew must paint the empty shell of a ship that is about to be made into scrap. The unconscious story is often the rest of the story.

STORY 9
THE WAREHOUSE

Bob, a recent business graduate, took a job in sales for a small candle manufacturer in a nearby state. He set about his work diligently and made many sales in the northern part of his state. This attracted the owner's interest since there were not a lot of pins representing customers in his wall-mounted map of the United States. He invited Bob to visit him and the plant.

When he arrived, Bob was given a tour of the plant and learned about all the intricacies of making candles. Any number of problems might arise that created unusable candles, such as wicks of the wrong type or size, wax improperly processed, scents that were off, and decorative finishes improperly applied. Following the plant tour he was walked through a huge warehouse with shelving twelve feet high. During the walk-through Bob, who was already quite familiar with the catalog, noticed a substantial amount of inventory that was not in the catalog. When he inquired, he was told the candles had defects and did not meet quality standards.

The next day he met with the owner, a surgeon who had been recruited to the area because it had few health-care providers. The surgeon owned not only the plant but also a car dealership that he said might soon go bankrupt because of a major embezzlement. As the meeting began, the owner was looking through a stack of index cards. He explained that he was financially strapped and that he had to find hundreds of thousands of dollars to build a new warehouse. The index cards were the names of patients who might be talked into having different types of elective surgery—the answer to his cash-flow problem.

Bob eventually mentioned to the surgeon-owner that the warehouse was full of spoiled inventory—about 40 percent, based on a quick count of linear shelf space that he had done in a few minutes after the tour. Bob suggested selling the inventory to the big discount store down the street for the cost of materials; then the surgeon would not have to build a warehouse, and he would in fact have a major cash infusion. The owner, being a surgeon, was dependent on his plant manager and a nearby university faculty member who served as a consultant to run the plant efficiently. He was surprised but also ecstatic about the possibilities, and he immediately told his sales manager to sell the spoiled inventory. In a few days the sale was made and the warehouse cleared out.

Bob returned home feeling as though he had made a timely contribution to problem solving. Within a week, however, he was informed that he was being terminated. When he asked the sales manager about this, he told Bob the idea to sell the spoiled inventory had embarrassed both the plant manager and the university professor-consultant. They had lost face with the owner and were furious. His head had to roll.

Questions

Why did at least three characters in this story not pursue rational enlightened self-interest?

Why was Bob, successful in his job, fired?

How do embarrassment, humiliation, and revenge trump rational economic decision making in this story?

In what ways did the surgeon's actual or operant values conflict with ideal physician values?

What were the roles and conflicts of the plant manager and faculty consultant in this story?

Discussion and Analysis

It is likely a truism that organizations often do not seek and achieve excellence. Striving to create better organizations, workplaces, business processes, and performance would *seem* to be an imperative and is often engraved in mission statements. However, accurate reality testing most often does not support these assumptions. Organizations are filled with interpersonal and group dynamics that are hard to understand, dysfunctional, and even more challenging to remediate.

The idea that organizations are primarily based on rational, objective, enlightened self-interest is a fondly held illusion. In the story, although the plant manager and university consultant wanted more profit, their obsession with their own images clearly trumped this ostensible goal. As a result they sabotaged their own business with poor management and by terminating their top-performing salesperson. The plant manager and the university consultant were driven to be rid of the person who had humiliated them—a vindictive triumph to restore fragile but arrogant pride.

Bob clearly was learning about business the hard way. The actual goals of these leaders of the organization were to look good and protect their overdetermined narcissism. It was important that their work and decisions not be held up for critical inspection. Any real or perceived deficiencies might harm their inflated sense of themselves. This was especially true relative to their employees, whom the managers probably saw as inferior to them—an outcome of splitting and projection. The employees were the cause of any problems. They created them.

As in this story, any damage to the arrogant pride of executives can produce an immediate vindictive response. The offender(s) had to be destroyed, the messenger killed. In this story the plant manager and university consultant did not experience Bob as a separate human being with needs of his own but strictly as a means to an end. Their transference became emotionally violent when Bob inadvertently reminded them that they were not measuring up to their idealized, omniscient, and omnipotent self-images.

The story also leaves one to wonder about health-care providers, in this case the surgeon. How often are patients regarded merely as a source of cash flow? In this case patients who might benefit in some way from elective surgery were seen as a source of cash. The tension between health-care delivery and making a profit is evident. Physicians, while ideally patient focused, often do not place patient care foremost in their thinking. This in turn leads them to rationalize their actions. In this scenario physicians view patients less as people meriting compassion and respect and more as objects through which income may be generated. This type of surgeon performs wallet biopsies (assessing how much money the patient has) as often as medical biopsies.

Finally, this story forces us to reconsider what people—not only organizational leaders—regard as their ultimate interest, *self-interest*. The dark side of life often overshadows the enlightened side of life—often to the destruction of organizations and the self-destruction of leaders. Bob's well-intentioned insights and suggestions led to his immediate demise, retribution for unintentionally harming the plant manager's and consultant's expansive but fragile egos.

STORY 10

No Exit

An organization with more than three thousand employees decided to downsize to reduce costs. A consulting company that specialized in downsizing was hired. It proceeded to apply industry benchmarking to locate the organizational fat. A few months passed while everyone watched and waited. Everyone knew. Everyone felt like they had a target on their back. Then one Friday morning the axe fell. Guards with lists circulated through the facility to escort those selected for termination to a small auditorium. They arrived carrying boxes of possessions. When they entered, guards closed the doors to the auditorium.

In the large room was a line of tables with human resources staff seated behind them. The line of more than a hundred employees—soon to be former employees—progressed down the line of tables, turning in keys and identity badges, receiving information, forms, and signing a few documents regarding severance pay, which was conditional upon saying nothing to anyone about their termination. When the termination process was finished, a guard escorted each employee to an emergency door that led to the parking lot. Left behind were many things—financial security, friends, self-worth, a sense of fair play, and in some ways the future.

A week later, during an interview with the CEO, who was Jewish, a consultant asked whether the CEO saw any similarities to what others had done on his behalf and the selections and processing in Nazi death camps during World War II. He pondered the question for a few seconds, then simply said no.

Questions

How is it that executives seize upon such inhumane methods, often enabled by specialized consultants who decide who is to stay and who is to be terminated, as well as the process of how it is to be handled?

Are they merely adopting the fad of the moment?

Are they simply following the recommendations of the consulting company?

Are they so well psychologically defended that laying off hundreds or thousands of employees is for them just business, lacking any sense of humanity?

In what way(s) might the CEO be reliving or repeating his and his family's past through the way the downsizing was executed?

Discussion and Analysis

A scene like this has become all too common when sweeping reengineering methods are adopted to create profound and immediate changes, often to manage stock values. Downsizing and layoffs, a common feature of the twenty-first-century workplace, produce sweeping devastation of individuals and local communities. Formerly high-performing executives and employees are transformed into the unemployed and can find no equivalent positions or none at all, depending on their age. Long-term unemployment, chronic underemployment, and forced retirement are now a part of the public discourse.

The answer to the questions that follow this story is likely "all the above." There are no easy answers. There is no easy way to avoid these outcomes once employees come to be seen as merely costs and disposable human resources. The CEO knew exactly what had happened but seemed oblivious and disconnected from what it really meant in terms of human lives or its possible relevance to his Jewish heritage. In particular the psychological defenses that CEOs and other executives may rely on should be examined. Certainly common defenses like rationalization and denial may come into play. Likewise a notion such as selective attention may play a role, with the executives paying attention on some level while ignoring or disregarding other aspects, leading to the sometimes implausible response of "I did not know." Certainly splitting and projection are important to consider as they can turn people into bad objects—organizational fat—that has to be removed. They in fact deserve to be terminated. Consider how depersonalizing even the term *human resources* is.

Another consideration is the devastating impact of downsizing and layoffs on both those who are terminated and those who stay, the survivors. Those who are suddenly terminated at least temporarily lose their career, financial well-being, ability to care for their families, sense of self-efficacy and worth, and trust in the old axiom that if they are loyal and work hard, they will be valued by their employer. They sometimes lose long friendships with colleagues they may never see again, and, if they do see them, the encounter can be awkward. Finding compassion for terminated friends is difficult when those same people remind the survivors how painful it is to be laid off. Better to unilaterally protect yourself by distancing yourself from those who are gone. Considerations like this are depressing, disillusioning, and sad. Life has irreversibly changed for the worse.

Those who remain often feel that they may well be next, as they work harder to handle the work of their departed colleagues as well as their own. In particular they may feel that, because they are so pressured to get everything done, the quality of their work is diminished, leading in turn to a profound sense of loss of the ability to take pride in their work. Employees may also suffer from survivor guilt as they pass by the empty desks and workstations.

Finally, layoffs are often large enough that local communities are affected. Community food banks become swamped by demand, as are other nonprofit and governmental services for the unemployed and poverty stricken. The loss of income in the community can lead to diminished business revenue, the closing of small and even large businesses, and the concomitant loss of even more jobs, thereby deepening the damage to the community.

In sum, downsizing leads to multiple results for people and communities: from the downsizing itself, the way the firing takes place, the aftermath of being fired in a downsizing, and the experience of being a survivor who is not fired. Everyone is traumatized. The story underscores how dehumanizing the process of downsizing can be. The expression "nothing personal, just business" masks how personal downsizing is for everyone involved.

STORY 11
STONES

Mike was a new senior manager of the central office for a dozen major divisions that marketed specialized services. Each division had its own manager and staff that submitted billing information to the central billing office. The office was run by Betty, who had been there more than a decade, working her way up to manager. Mike found a deeply entrenched "us versus them" mentality between the central office and the dozen divisions. The animosity was strong, and it had been present for so many years it had become taken for granted. It was just the way things were.

Mike saw that this situation was creating losses of income in the millions of dollars and had to be addressed. He asked Betty to chair a group that included the dozen division administrators, and the group's goal was to solve the many billing problems. Betty agreed, although she was reluctant to take on the job because of the long history of animosity between her office and the other divisions. Mike called the first meeting and pointed out to the group how much revenue was being lost and that this was avoidable. Fixing the problem would be a win-win. He gave the group a name, the Billing Assault Team, to emphasize the importance of fixing the billing problems. He then left the meeting with Betty in charge.

Mike asked Betty later how the rest of the meeting had gone. Betty said she was relieved that everyone there had not attacked her. After the second meeting she said they were beginning to make some progress. After the fourth meeting she entered Mike's office in tears. She reported that during the meeting everyone addressed the long history of animosity and realized all of it was unnecessary and that they actually enjoyed working together and with Betty. She said the meeting had been cathartic, and everyone had a sense of hope things would get better.

A few weeks later Mike walked into Betty's office and found a number of rubber bats for Halloween hanging from her ceiling. She said they symbolized the team spirit of the new work group, whose acronym was BAT.

Mike eventually moved on to manage an even larger billing office in another organization that had even more specialized divisions. Each also submitted billing to a central system that he managed, and once again there was a dysfunctional history spanning several decades. In this case the combative relationship between the divisions and the central office was highly energized. The divisions constantly criticized the billing office, which was well armed with the entire history of the problems in the divisions and had a large database weaponized for counterattack. Shortly after he began his new job, Mike asked the managers in the billing office to disarm. No more stone throwing in response to being attacked. They had to stop fighting back. The managers did not want to do this. Mike asked them to try it for a few weeks, which they were willing to do. They unilaterally disarmed.

A few weeks later the senior manager of the office commented at a meeting how much better she and her colleagues felt about themselves. They had taken the high road and felt they were doing the right thing by not retaliating against those who criticized them, even though they continued to be attacked. Over several months the constant attacks on the billing office diminished. It seemed as though all the fun had been drained from combat when one side simply stopped fighting.

Questions

Why is it so hard at times to break a cycle of violence—attack and counterattack?

In reducing the level of organizational violence, how important is it for everyone involved to humanize both sides of the conflict?

What kind of interpersonal, intergroup, and organizational dynamics tend to contribute to creating groups that others want to attack?

What role can leadership play in terms of avoiding, minimizing, and stopping conflict in the workplace?

Why did the staffs feel better when they stopped throwing stones?

Discussion and Analysis

These stories speak to the remarkable persistence of dysfunctional organizational dynamics over time, even when it is easily demonstrated large sums of revenue are being lost. What seems important is the joy of the game, and it becomes evident that the battle and its persistence signal it has come to be taken for granted. These dynamics are also encouraged by psychological dynamics such as splitting and projection, where each side is certain that the other side is bad and wrong. Knowing this then authorizes the continuous attacks from both sides. These dynamics are further aggravated by ongoing narcissistic injuries to leaders on both sides. Everyone becomes a loser. The intensity of these feelings is further inflamed by transference from past experience that in turn creates feelings and actions in the present that are disproportionate to the provocation (sometimes called hot buttons). Breaking this reinforcing cycle of organizational destruction is challenging but also not that hard to accomplish when one side ceases its counterattacks.

The underlying questions are why, under some circumstances—from organizational to international—these oppositional organizational dynamics continue and rigidify? And, second, why do people seem to melt into tears of gratitude, relief, and reconciliation when the combatants are drawn together in a place safe enough to allow them to reflect on their actions? What makes the difference in terms of learning from experience to end vicious self-defeating cycles of interpersonal and organizational pathology and mutual recrimination? Part of the answer lies in the quality and unconscious of the leader. In these stories Mike's character proved to be the crucial ingredient, when in the first story he asked the managers to come together to solve the billing problems and in the second story when he asked the managers in the billing office to unilaterally disarm.

Decades of psychopolitical work by Vamik Volkan (1988, 1997, 2001, 2004, 2005, 2006) and his colleagues has shown that when historical enemies can—in the presence of empathic facilitators—allow themselves to be vulnerable during meetings, both sides can acknowledge their fears and vulnerabilities and recognize the stereotypes they erect to fend these off. They can begin to lower their shields. The stories clearly illustrate that this appreciation applies equally well to organizations. It is possible to change deeply embedded dysfunctional organizational dynamics when leaders create a context in which these patterns of behavior are openly questioned. Leaders can play an active role in making the workplace and meetings safe enough for everyone to take time to reflect. What are we doing here? This safe time and space created by the leader may then encourage a more trusting, open, and collaborative approach to mutual problem solving that benefits everyone and the organization.

STORY 12
WHAT'S WRONG WITH THIS PICTURE?

Micah is an administrator in a large academic department in a medical school that is organizationally separate from its teaching hospital. He met with the hospital's recently hired chief financial officer, Jay, about missed billing opportunities for the hospital. While conducting a professional fee billing audit of a clinical lab at a remote site, Micah's billing staff found billing opportunities the clinical faculty had missed and a 100 percent failure by the hospital to bill for activity at this site. This amounted to many hundreds of thousands of dollars of lost revenue for the hospital every year, and fixing the problem was easy.

Jay was sitting at a desk covered with several foot-high stacks of computer reports and listened without much comment and no questions. Weeks later Micah was called to a meeting with Jay and several of his recently hired staff members. Once again Micah explained the problem. Everyone listened and asked only a few clarifying questions. A number of weeks passed and another meeting was scheduled. This time Jay had four staff members at the meeting. Many were also new hires. Micah again explained the problem and got the same response. At yet a third meeting Micah found eight members of Jay's staff. Micah was beginning to suspect Jay's goal was to intimidate him by having ever larger numbers of staff members attend these sessions. Micah also was starting to wonder whether the goal was to get him to drop the inquiry, thereby making the problem go away. During this third meeting it became clear that Jay and all of his staff did not even know they had a clinical lab at the site—one explanation for why there was no billing and a likely by-product of Jay's hiring all new staff. Months passed and nothing changed. Jay called no subsequent meetings.

Eventually Micah wrote the billing opportunity up as a suggestion and submitted it to the suggestion award program, which required a written response. The suggestion was accompanied by detailed documentation, including how much lost billing had occurred since the first meeting and how to fix the problem. Micah won an award for this suggestion. After a few more months the problem was fixed.

Questions

What does it *feel* like to be Micah and Jay?

Why did Jay not do the obvious and use Micah's findings to proceed with billing?

What would Jay stand to *lose* if he accepted Micah's findings about missed billing opportunities? (The organization obviously would *gain* money.)

Why did Jay stonewall Micah's attempt to bring financial reality to Jay's attention?

What does Micah's alternate approach, submitting the billing opportunity to the hospital's suggestion award program, say about his orientation to reality?

Discussion and Analysis

What you don't know *can* hurt you (financially), but acknowledging that you don't know can cause (public) embarrassment for a leader, especially one who is somewhat arrogant (covering insecurity). Therefore, following this logic, intimidation and saving face are preferable to accurate reality testing and acknowledging the presence of problems, even if it means losing hundreds of thousands of dollars. The fiscal health of the hospital seems to have been less important than avoiding tarnishing the self-image of the CFO and his staff.

Occasionally perseverance pays off. Micah knew one way (maybe the only way) to force the CFO to acknowledge and fix the billing problem, and that was to send a written recommendation to the suggestion award committee. One lesson here is the importance of knowing the organizational culture and its channels and how to use them effectively to get things done, even though that may entail some personal risk on occasion. Challenging authority can be, and often is, a threatening and even career-ending move.

It is perhaps an illusion or delusion that the senior executives of an institution are on top of everything. Can they be expected to know about all aspects of their organization? Clearly the new CFO and his staff in this story did not know they had this clinical lab where their physicians were performing services for the hospital's patients. One would want to think that a CFO and certainly his staff would know something as basic as where all their facilities are. They had plenty of time to learn it between the meetings.

Also to be considered is the difference between a CFO brought in from the outside, who knows nothing about the organization, and one who worked his way up through the ranks of a hospital and knows the organization, its people, and its culture. In this case Jay was brought in as a turnaround artist from another hospital, as was the case for many of his staff. Jay knew hospital financial management, but he did not know this hospital. A few of these staff members were even from different industries and knew little or nothing about medicine and hospital administration. Whatever else could be said about Andrew Carnegie's interpersonal skills (and his treatment of his vast supply of coal and steel workers in the early twentieth century), he knew coal, coke, iron, and steel from years of hands-on experience.

New CEOs and upper management are often brought into organizations with great fanfare and the frequent expectation that they will almost magically solve the financial and operating problems attributed to previous management. In cases like this, the "all good" new contrasts with the "all bad" old. Indeed, if new upper managers do not already possess some grandiosity, their hyped introduction as saviors will induce it. They can easily become arrogant and ultimately defensive of their inflated sense of their own competence and self-importance.

New executives often throw out the past. The leaders and employees they replace may be held up for contempt and scapegoated as the source of all the problems. However, if organizational memory is lost when the original leaders and employees are terminated or leave, no one can learn from the past, some of which is invariably of value. New executives often arrogantly do not take advantage of at least listening to how things used to work, even if they did not work well. They may well then repeat what has not worked well in the past (and for good reasons), and they may not see all the possibilities within their new organization for how to improve it. In particular they may not listen to remaining employees with many years of experience, who are disregarded as part of the problem. The self-importance, arrogance, and disregard for the past and others sets the new crew up to encounter avoidable difficulties and even failures as they go about reinventing the organization to fit their grand design. Should failure arise again, and new management be hired yet again, they may well repeat the mistakes all over again. This creates a cycle of less-than-successful change, as well as disbelief on the part of long-term employees, who are both ignored and forced to witness recurrent problems arising from not knowing the organization and from ill-considered decisions and implementations of solutions.

STORY 13

PUMPKIN DAY

Marcy was recently hired by Eric, a new senior-level executive, to manage a ninety-person staff that operated a large information system. The recent history was horrific. A long-serving dysfunctional executive had been forced out along with the director Marcy replaced. Morale was exceedingly poor. A set of employee interviews conducted by a consultant revealed seriously bad conditions, which the consultant summarized as the employees' experiencing the department as a sweatshop and a prison.

The sweatshop atmosphere arose from the failure to provide raises for the previous three years and from cramming staff members into work cubicles measuring three feet by two feet. Their chairs were so close to those behind them that they frequently bumped. The sense of its being a prison came from a long list of oppressive rules about appearance, what could be eaten at one's desk (this included sweeps of desk drawers for contraband items), and a prohibition against talking to each other in nearby lounges. Given the many oppressive and detailed rules, the supervisors responsible for enforcing them essentially acted like prison guards.

After reviewing the findings with Eric and agreeing on how to approach them, Marcy posted a list of twenty significant complaints and issues gleaned from the interviews to make clear that she had heard what her staff thought and felt. She then proceeded to remediate these problems. Some could be handled immediately, such as tearing up the lists of behavioral mandates and directing supervisors to stop acting like prison guards. Marcy also provided more resources to support the staff in doing their work. With the support of upper management Eric and Marcy assembled a task group to review wages that were set at or near the minimum wage. This led to significant increases in pay to levels consistent with the positions and their responsibilities.

By October Marcy had made great progress, fueled by her enthusiasm, high energy level, great interpersonal skills, and her technical knowledge of her staff's work. She had become a transformational leader in a matter of a few months. The staff asked whether they could celebrate Halloween by wearing costumes—something that was inconceivable to even contemplate with the old managers. Marcy agreed and provided decorations and suitably seasonal food for a luncheon.

The Halloween celebration was a landmark departure from the oppression of the previous decade or more. Many of the costumes and make-up were outstanding. Everyone enjoyed the new sense of respect and freedom.

Questions

How did Eric and Marcy change the oppressive work atmosphere created by the previous executive and director?

In what ways does the previous management exemplify workplace bullying?

What was the role of upper management in Marcy's success?

How did the Halloween costumes serve as a symbol of the new management style?

How did Eric's support set the stage for Marcy's leadership style and its success?

Discussion and Analysis

This is a story with two sides. One side is a story about how executives, managers, and supervisors can turn the workplace into a sweatshop and prison. The level of oppression and management by fear and intimidation was remarkable. That ninety employees, many of whom had been there many years, were able to tolerate this for so long is also remarkable.

A context like this, filled with us-versus-them dynamics, is fueled by splitting and projection. Staff came to feel that people in leadership roles are all bad or nearly so, beliefs reinforced by abusive and oppressive actions that are so common as to be routine. Similarly the executive in charge and the managers saw employees as not having common sense, needing close watching and control, and not meriting respect or adequate compensation. The managers saw themselves as good and the employees as bad and therefore deserving of punishment and sadistic handling. This led to a polarizing organizational split that lasted many years. Under these circumstances anger and aggression go underground for the most part. Calling an organizational context like this into question is often not survivable, especially when terminations for rule violations are a regular occurrence. If you need the income and benefits, you learn to persevere.

The other side to the story speaks to hope and human resilience. With Eric's support, Marcy kicked over the cans of worms by posting the list of problems on the bulletin board. She made public the private suffering and made the undiscussable experience of working there open to inspection and repair. A willingness to do this in a leadership role is an awesome thing. It is filled with many unknown and hard-to-contemplate dynamics that can create losses of control. Marcy was ultimately dependent on the goodwill of the staff to not create a crisis as she opened up for discussion the long history of workplace oppression. The words *courage* and *grace* come to mind.

Marcy's confronting the list demonstrated good faith and her respect for and trust in the staff. She allowed herself to be vulnerable. She also had to engage in a leap of faith that Eric and upper management would stand by her as she drained the swamp. She also had to stand aside, much like a participant-observer, and not engage in the splitting and projection that had been so omnipresent in the former management group relative to the staff. She had to act to contain these dynamics as well as the anxiety, fear, aggression, shame, and loss of how things used to be that many were feeling.

In sum, she had to believe in herself, her boss, the change process the two had designed, and her ability to make it happen while containing the many potentially destructive interpersonal and group dynamics that exposed the decade-long oppression. The pumpkin pie served for Halloween was a hard-won prize for everyone.

From a different perspective Eric's support of Marcy in making these challenging changes seems important. He not only offered her support, but he covered her back in an organization filled with hostility towards her area of responsibility. Eric also was willing to support financially the findings of the salary task group, which made it clear that staff raises were in order.

Finally, the process of obtaining permission for, planning, and holding the Halloween party can be viewed as a metaphor for the change in emotional atmosphere. The Halloween party introduced play, playfulness, and spontaneity into a department formerly marked by drudgery and enforced routine. Together Eric and Marcy created a new "potential space" in which people could be trusted and could trust in themselves to be valued for their contribution to the work. The generation of new ideas and solutions to problems could take place without fear of punishment. Perhaps the sense of fright was thereafter limited to Halloween.

Conclusion

We and others we know have spent much of our working lives encountering organizational dynamics similar to these stories. These experiences are, we suggest, commonplace and underappreciated in terms of their omnipresence and of the organizational and personal harm they do. They also are often exceptionally resistant to change, even when the harm is documented and reported by employees, who fear they may become the messenger who will be killed off. Even the expendable organizational consultant may not be bold enough to forfeit fees and profit for accurate reality testing and honest feedback. We appreciate that it takes courage to face a dysfunctional reality that may dominate an organization to everyone's harm. Who is willing to say that the emperor has no clothes or risk being attacked and discredited by a gang in the workplace, when the actions of a division or section are held up for scrutiny? In the politics of the United States and other democracies, how common are denial, generation of misleading and even untrue assertions and facts, personal attacks to discredit someone, and the energetic pursuit of a scapegoat to blame?

Often there are no easy answers when a new leader, employee, or consultant encounters these dynamics. Likewise, it seems as though this is the way the organization members want it or even like it—or that the level of threat and oppression by the leader and others is so powerful that it suppresses even thinking about change. The very thought of change can simply be too dangerous. These dysfunctional dynamics are familiar and often are defended out of fear of change, as reflected in the idea of sticking with the devil you know. Successful change cannot even be contemplated absent a (preferably systemic) readiness for change embraced at least within semiautonomous divisions, lest it lead directly to vindictive responses. In a sense there must be sufficient organizational pain and suffering to consider change, where the threat of change is not perceived to be worse than doing nothing. We suggest that doing nothing is sometimes not a viable option, especially if the organization is failing to thrive or altogether failing.

In sum, the ability to contemplate and make change may arise only where the sense of threat is greater than the actual or fantasized threat of change. This is often true of top-down change that is rammed through the organization, sometimes by a charismatic new CEO or outside consultants. Resisting the CEO is more distressing than the threat of change. Given the widespread existence of similar organizational dynamics, we advocate for a need to understand readiness for change as much as the need for change itself.

We now turn our attention to the dark side of organizational dysfunction where sometimes buildings are left standing but many of the employees are vanished—perhaps leaving a shadow, not unlike the human shadows cast by the vaporized human beings in Hiroshima and Nagasaki. Offices and furniture remain, but the invisible presence of the employees who were there yesterday is all that remains in the hearts and minds of those who survived a layoff and now must do their work and the work of others no longer present.

CHAPTER 7

The Geography of Organizational Darkness

Introduction

The stories in this chapter are about the experience of organizational space and the conscious and unconscious meaning or construction of space, including even the design and occupation of new space in an organization. It is about organizational space as symbol and metaphor and symbolic space as ritualized. A CEO's door may come to symbolize the CEO's recurrent intimidation of unsuspecting visitors in the office.

In these scenarios a desk is not simply a surface on which to work. A chair is not simply a place in which to sit. An empty office is not simply a work space that awaits a new occupant. A new building is not simply a place in which to get work done. Rather they are places that are suffused with and embody personal and shared (group) desires, fantasies, wishes, feelings, and defenses, both conscious and unconscious. Organizational space is not neutral. Organizational space often plays out the dark side of organizational life. This will become clear with the stories in this chapter.

None of this should be surprising. Put differently, the stories will remind readers of what they already know but perhaps have not put into words. The flip side of virtually any instrumental, utilitarian object in the workplace is expressive, that is, filled with human meaning and feeling. However, because we tend to think of workplaces and organizations in strictly rational-technical terms, as places in which to perform work, we overlook the obvious. The stories illustrate how important it is for organizational leaders, managers, employees, researchers, scholars, and consultants to take psychogeography (Stein, 2013; Stein & Niederland, 1989) seriously.

STORY I
THE DESK

Being hired into a senior-level executive role is always a new adventure, often filled with learning what you thought is not the case. Take, for example, being hired as a vice president to replace a retiring executive, Bob, who had been in the position for thirty years. Almost immediately the new vice president, Frank, learned that Bob was retiring because he was being forced out by the new president. Bob, it turned out, was generally liked as a person but hated in his role of vice president because of his nearly absolute control of every facet of the organization's operations. He personally screened most of the purchases made everywhere within the $100 million, 750-employee organization, and he controlled the budgets and all operations. Bob was a micromanager, and if you crossed him, he would make your life so miserable you would voluntarily leave. He seldom had to fire anyone.

Frank overlapped with Bob for a month or so and shared Bob's office with him. Bob invited Frank to spread out his work on his desk, which he found stacked neatly on a chair every morning. Bob's going-away dinner had a life-sized cardboard figure of him dressed in a black suit and fedora and holding a huge white coffee mug with BOSS printed on it in large letters. It was not clear whether this was a playful approach to Bob and his tenure or something else. Either way it was striking.

After Bob departed, Frank had the office to himself. Frank's experience of this space was how Bob's huge desk dominated the space. The desk had two large extensions that made it a U shape. The desk filled the room, leaving only a four-foot space around the desk. Eight armless metal chairs were lined up against the walls—four in front and four to the right side of the desk. The left side of the desk was near a window, and it was a few feet from the back wall, so it was possible to walk around the desk to enter the U. Frank's experience of the desk was one of sitting in a commanding position, with everything and everyone else in the space diminished, relegated to the thin strip of small chairs on two sides. Add to this a large high-backed chair, and the feeling was one of power, dominance, and mastery—a lord of the universe. When Frank replaced the desk with modern office furniture in the corner opposite the door to the room, the room turned out to be large and easily accommodated a small conference table for meetings. The office also gained a welcoming sense of openness.

Questions

To the person entering Bob's office, does the place feel closed or open?

What kind of power relations does the space induce or conjure in the person entering the office?

How can the space be understood to be a projection of the executive?

From the feeling generated upon entering the office, what kind of relationship or interaction does the person anticipate?

What does a work space say about the occupant and to the person entering that space?

Discussion and Analysis

The two contrasting descriptions of the *use* of the office space illustrate workplace psychogeography. The story illustrates how the occupant's personality and preferred style of relationships are played out in the use of space, including what is put where and the size of the artifacts. It would almost be possible to read an executive's personality in the layout and relative size of furniture and other objects in the room. Office—and wider workplace—space is personally experienced and not simply as functional or instrumental (tools to get work done). Further, the person occupying the office structures the office space to give, or induce, an experience to or in whoever comes in.

The story suggests several questions that could be applied to the two office arrangements. Does the person entering the office feel small (diminished, excluded) or life-sized (welcomed)? More generally all the attributes of an organization can be used to project such aspects of the leader's personality as power, importance, creativity, or even minimization of importance. One's experience of a building and how it and its offices are designed and decorated influence what one expects to find upon entering the building or office. Power furniture is not a new idea, and the notion behind it extends to how buildings are designed and decorated. This appreciation helps those who enter buildings, floors, and offices to be aware of the sense of the space and what is being communicated. Appreciating the conscious and unconscious experience is critically important.

The executive suite often sends a clear message to all those who enter. Nice carpet over a thick pad, large expensive desks occupied by secretaries and administrative assistants, and nice wall art accented by bullet lights all send a message. All this is evident before you take more than a few steps into the suite. Some who enter feel less important or significant. You feel diminished and even vulnerable to the sense of power conveyed. Taking the time to look closely at the space and objects, and the experience they generate, is important in terms of locating what is being communicated, perceived, or experienced. Being aware gives you a moment to pause and reflect and perhaps restore your own significance if it was diminished. For organizational consultants the awareness provides insights in terms of working with the CEO and executives and their staff members as well as the organization as a whole.

STORY 2

THE EMPTY OFFICE

While consulting with a computer company, an organizational consultant, Robert, interviewed one of the company's financial managers, Joan. The subject was her experience of a recent downsizing. Joan was almost out of breath as she spoke. Robert could hear panic in her voice. Her story goes as follows:

> Am I glad to see you today! Robert, the strangest thing happened on Monday. I was off sick on Friday. I came in to work on Monday morning, and the office next to me was cleared out. There was a desk, a chair, a computer, a couple of file cabinets and bookcases, a wastebasket. And that's it. Empty. I still can't believe it, and it's

already Friday. It's like there's a big hole in this place. I knew the guy ten years. His name is Don. He was one of our number crunchers. A quiet guy who just did his work. It seemed like he was always here, always working. He is a computer whiz, and anyone in the unit could go to him about a computer glitch. We aren't—maybe I should say *weren't*, since he's gone—weren't exactly friends, but we worked together on a lot of projects. He was kind of part of the furniture.

It's so eerie. I'm numb over it. I keep going next door to look in his office, expecting to see him. Maybe I'm imagining that he's gone, and he's not. But the place is *so* empty. I've heard of this kind of thing happening in other places when people get RIFed [RIF stands for reduction in force]. Here today, gone tomorrow. But I've not heard of this here. It's like he disappeared. It is as though he was never here. Robert, I'm not being sentimental about him. He and I didn't have something going—if you're thinking that. I just can't believe they'd do it—and the *way* they did it. I asked around the firm, and everybody gave the same story. It wasn't just him. It happened all over the place. About five hundred people were RIFed in one day.

I asked around, and nobody knows where Don went. There is no forwarding address or telephone number. It's weird, Robert. He just disappeared. You wonder if you're next. You try not to think of it. Work harder, maybe they'll keep you. It's ridiculous, because you know it's not true. But you've got to believe that you're valuable to them.

Questions

When downsizing occurs, who are the victims? Is it those who lose their jobs or those who stay and usually have to absorb the work their former colleagues performed?

Do survivors of downsizing experience survivor's guilt and post-traumatic stress?

How are events like this remembered? Are the events as recalled changed or soon forgotten?

How do those who are left cope with the possibility that they might be next?

How should adjustments in staffing levels be handled to avoid the experience of the empty office?

Discussion and Analysis

Events and experiences like this have occurred many millions of times in American workplaces. When they occur, forms of "managed social change"—variously called RIFs, downsizing, rightsizing, redundancy, outsourcing, off-shoring, separation, deskilling, restructuring, and re-engineering— give those who are fired no warning or preparation, except perhaps through gossip and rumor. These massive changes are experienced as terrifying, dehumanizing, traumatizing attacks. Sometimes they occur as unexpected letters of dismissal in the U.S. Mail or as e-mail. Sometimes they take the guise of a fire drill, when everyone is supposed to leave the building, and those who are summarily fired are not allowed back in after the false drill is over.

However the firings are executed, they are designed to maximize surprise, if not terror, and to achieve a clean break of those who remain from those who are cast away as dead wood. They psychologically terrorize the workplace. People are suddenly and efficiently disappeared. One thinks of parallels with the *desaparacidos* (the disappeared ones) in Argentina in the "dirty wars" of the 1980s, when members of the militia would whisk someone away, and that person was never seen again. In downsizing, there are no metaphoric bodies to see and step over, no blood spilled. Downsizing is symbolic murder, what Leonard Shengold (1991) called "soul murder." The carnage is attested to by sudden and large-scale absence, void. Those who remain are left with only images in mind. The symbolic kill is swift and clean. Work is expected to continue within this empty shell. The past is repudiated as bad and worthless; the present and future are held up as good and promising.

From this story it should be clear that the psychological experience (psychological reality) of the workplace, and of its space, is part of the workplace, not some inconsequential epiphenomenon. For instance, the office adjacent to Joan's was not the only one empty in the company; there were many empty offices. It is likely that the experience of having an empty office next door is different from knowing that offices are empty *somewhere else* in the building. And for Joan an office full of furniture was nonetheless empty.

This story also raises the question of who are the victims of downsizing? Most outsiders regard only those who have been fired to be the victims. Yet, as this story testifies, the survivors, those who remain behind with jobs, are equally victims. The survivors are burdened with keeping the workplace running. Fearing that they might be the next to be fired, the survivors often feel as if they have targets on their backs. They must do not only their own jobs but also the jobs of those who were fired—with no increase in pay, only increases in responsibility. They are overworked, underpaid, and haunted.

We wonder how long Don will be remembered, even by Joan. Managers and executives exert immense pressure on employees to forget about those who are gone, to not mention them by name, to forget even that they ever worked there. All these can be seen as defenses, both individual and social, on the part of those who remain. If those who are gone do not exist and do not deserve to be remembered, then (as the psychological logic goes) those who remain need not feel loss, grief, or guilt. Instead, everyone must move on, work hard, always appear busy, and keep a low profile. They try to persuade themselves that they are valuable, perhaps even indispensable, to the company, though they also live in constant fear that they will be the next to be eliminated.

The experience of seeing other employees disappear is terrifying in the context of the expectation that one is working in a civilized workplace. Employees who survive a RIF try to protect themselves from psychotic anxiety, separation panic, and surreal feelings of depersonalization and flashes of derealization (a feeling of altered reality). The downsizing was too close for comfort. Employees try in various ways to distance the event—and the people who were fired—from themselves. After all, the people who still have jobs experienced a brush with (symbolic) mortality. Many survivors feel "there but for the grace of G-d go I." Some employees improvise stories such as "They must have done *something* to get fired" (a supposition that serves as protection from the intolerable idea of seemingly random firings). Many employees experience survivor guilt and ask, "Why was I spared?" In turn they try to protect themselves from overwhelming guilt by making up stories about how they must be essential to the company.

Meanwhile, Joan is left in a panic. Fortunately she has Robert, the consultant, to talk with—at least for a while—and to help her contain her anxiety, emptiness, and fear. Most others are not so lucky.

STORY 3

MUSICAL CHAIRS

Tom has been hired to replace Dick, a senior-level executive who held the position for fifteen years. It was clear to Tom from the start that Dick had been forced out because of a large number of complaints about how he used his power and information to control and dominate the organization. Many of his immediate staff had also left or were leaving, creating a management void because no one was being replaced. In a brief conversation a former close associate of Dick's volunteered to Tom that Dick really loved to be hated.

One morning as part of getting started, Tom had a meeting scheduled with Jill, an MBA who managed a large department, to start talking about how they would work together. When Jill arrived for the appointment, the door was open, and Tom was on the phone. He briefly interrupted the call to greet Jill and invited her to sit down at the small conference table in the office. As Tom worked toward ending the call, he noticed Jill was still standing and once again invited her to sit down. After several minutes the call concluded, and Jill was still standing. As Tom approached the table a short distance from his desk, Jill appeared to be noticeably edgy. Tom once again asked her to sit down as he approached. Jill stood still. She then asked where Tom was going to sit, and he replied, "Anywhere." Jill still would not sit down. Tom finally grabbed a chair, and Jill immediately also sat down. She eventually shared with Tom that Dick had "his" chair, and she had once unknowingly sat down in his chair when she was new to the organization. This led to an outraged response and public humiliation, something to forever be avoided in the future.

A week or so later Tom had a meeting with Fran, who had canceled several times. Fran appeared at the door, and Tom greeted her and invited Fran to sit down, but she would not enter the room. A second invitation yielded the same results. Fran said she simply could not tolerate entering the room that still had all of Dick's power furniture in it. She asked to meet in a nearby conference room. She also eventually shared the reason in the safe space of the neutral conference room.

She had been Dick's administrative assistant for a number of years. When she decided to accept a higher-level position, Dick was enraged at what he considered her betrayal and abandonment. After she assumed her new role, Dick for many years conducted an intense personal vendetta that left her feeling vulnerable, threatened, and eventually an emotionally exhausted survivor, especially at those times she had to come to Dick's office.

Several weeks later Tom was eating the lunch at his small conference table with his office door closed. He heard what sounded like an explosion, and the walls and ceiling shook. This was followed by a second explosion, but this time Tom, now fully alert, realized that it was coming from the closed door. He cautiously opened the door, and there stood Harry, who also managed a large department. He had pounded exceptionally hard on the door. When Tom greeted him, his fist unclenched and his intense posture relaxed. Tom reflected in the moment that if sitting down at a table or merely entering the office was foreboding, the closed door must have been unbearable for Harry. Later Tom learned some of the history.

Harry had for years been attacked by Dick and attacked him in return. Neither could take the other out until Harry and a number of his colleagues grouped together to convince the CEO that Dick had to go. Pounding on the door, then, was a way of acting on the intense rage Harry felt for Dick that arose from an accumulation of narcissistic injuries over many years.

Questions

Do toxic leaders create toxic organizations?

How resilient are organization members?

How should organization members protect themselves from leaders like Dick?

Why do leaders like Dick often hold on to their positions for years, if not decades?

How might a consultant successfully coach or guide a leader like Dick?

Discussion and Analysis

This story is an example of a terrorized workplace. Even though the hateful and feared senior executive, Dick, is gone, his memory haunts the workplace and employees' relationships with his successor, Tom. This is a clear example of transference from previous (bad) relationships to current relationships: the present relives the past. It must be difficult for Tom to be Tom, since people experience him and respond to him as if he were Dick.

When Jill insisted on standing until Tom sat down in a chair he chose, and when Fran refused even to enter Tom's office, instead of reacting defensively Tom realized that Jill and Fran were not reacting to him (since they had no history with him), and something else must be going on. He was curious and inquisitive. Likewise with Harry, who had pounded on Tom's closed office door, Tom didn't take Harry's wrath as the result of something Tom had done but as a symbol and symptom of something else—how intimidating the previous occupant had been.

Put another way, Tom was making organizational assessments and a diagnosis based on employees' responses to him. Overcoming the past was clearly going to be the challenge. An even more general point to this story is that any new executive (or employee, for that matter) does not entirely "start fresh" based on his or her own merits but inherits attitudes, feelings, fantasies, and behaviors that were evoked by and directed toward his or her predecessor. Employees act toward a new executive at least in part as if the new boss were someone else.

The story also gives multiple examples of organizational psychogeography, that is, the psychodynamic construction and perception of space. The chairs in Tom's office, the office itself, and the closed door all served as psychogeographic symbols that Tom implicitly understood, and this understanding allowed him to respond appropriately to employees rather than defensively. Put differently: under ordinary circumstances a chair is something to sit down in, an office is to be entered, and a door may simply be opened. In this story the overwhelming and negative symbolic values of a chair, doorway, or door associated with horrific experiences with Dick tell a different story. Little is as it appears.

STORY 4
GOOD FENCES MAKE GOOD NEIGHBORS

In the heady experimental days of the 1960s and 1970s, a dean who had just been recruited to his college of liberal arts was put in charge of designing a new building to house the humanities departments, such as history, languages, sociology, anthropology, philosophy, and English, under one roof. He worked closely with architects to create a dream school. The dean's ideal workplace would be a place of no barriers.

The dean was an advocate of interdisciplinary studies. No longer would faculty be isolated in individual disciplinary kingdoms and fiefdoms. He envisioned a world of no boundaries and of fertile collaboration across humanities and social science disciplines. Departments would no longer be physically isolated from each other, and neither would the faculty. Faculty and others would have no closed offices, no walls, and no doors. In its place would be an open space with no boundaries or barriers. The dean hoped that this would enable everyone to unearth new opportunities and create new ideas with their many colleagues. Everyone would be connected with everyone else.

The dean's hope was that this open space itself would create an atmosphere of nearly infinite possibility. The dean imagined that it would encourage productivity not only within traditional disciplines but also among the disciplines, creating collaborative research and publications as well as teaching across fields. *Innovation, integration,* and *openness* were the buzzwords of the day.

The building opened with great fanfare, hope, and expectation. The festive atmosphere included a lavish buffet for everyone. By standing in front of a faculty member's desk, it was possible to look out and see virtually the entire school of liberal arts. The first months saw increased visiting throughout the immense room. Many projects began with the most unlikely collaborations.

Soon, however, a strange phenomenon occurred in the space. Faculty and staff slowly began arranging their bookcases, file cabinets, desks, chairs, tables, and other office furniture into enclosures or at least semi-enclosures. People positioned their desks and chairs so that they would see, and be seen by, fewer people. Entire departments restored their separateness through the strategic use of furniture. Soon the wide open spaces were replaced by improvised closed spaces that reintroduced the geography of the traditional departments and individual offices. Almost imperceptibly, prefabricated partitions gradually began to appear. So did partially enclosed modules. Some places actually began to resemble cubicles.

The dean was mystified. He found that he could not persuade or bully the faculty, staff, and departments into fulfilling his original dream. He could not make things happen, even though he was brought to the university to do precisely that. He was puzzled that his dream was not also theirs. Faculty and staff said that, in such totally open space, it was difficult to concentrate and get work done. It was impossible to have confidential telephone conversations or meetings. They had no sense of privacy; rather, people felt a pervasive sense of being observed all the time. As time passed, the old school of liberal arts was largely replicated within the huge room.

After so promising a beginning, the dean's dream building had become his nightmare. After five years of seeing his grand idea eroded and lost, he left to take a position elsewhere.

Questions

In planning the design of the new building, what was the dean's greatest mistake?

What role did the dean's overestimation of his own abilities play in his plan's downfall?

Who are the stakeholders in the building design and implementation?

What role(s) did boundaries play in the unfolding of the story?

How did the faculty and staff respond to the dean's ideal of no boundaries?

If you had been the dean, how would you have approached the design and spatial use of the new building?

Discussion and Analysis

This story offers a vivid illustration of the psychological linkages between individual, organization, and (American) society. It is also a poignant study in organizational resistance to change. The new dean had been given the mandate for change by the equally new provost and president. The university had invested millions of dollars in a new building and in the wager that this immense change in the way the department of liberal arts operated would be eagerly embraced by faculty and staff. The dean's ambition and grandiosity were matched and fanned by those who brought him in. So what went wrong?

The era in which this all took place was one of great hopes and expectations for change on the part of millions of Americans. It was a time of ideologies of integration, as expressed in no boundaries or limits. It was also a time in America that promoted extreme ideologies that set the stage for subsequent and often violent reactions. The new dean and his plans were brought in on the crest of a vast wave of change. Personality, organizational leadership, and a widespread ethos mirrored and fueled each other. The new dean had been given carte blanche by his superiors. Nothing was going to stand in the way of his vision.

Then, along the way, came the quiet but indomitable insurrection by the department chairs, faculty, and staff. They insisted on returning the college of liberal arts to the old way of relating and functioning. The use of the huge open space became a struggle between the old and familiar and the new elements of an ideology of no limits. The dean's major problem was that he had not given enough thought to the change process before making such extensive changes. He had been empowered by his superiors and the governing board. He, however, unwisely acted unilaterally and did not work with the people under him. Ultimately he could not sell his vision of a future with no limits and no boundaries to create interdisciplinary collaboration.

The new dean's first mistake—if it can be called that—was his failure to understand or realize that all change is accompanied by feelings of mourning for the loss of the familiar and traditional. This sense of loss, if not recognized and addressed by leadership, can readily unleash a strong rejection of the loss that is being imposed from the top down, sometimes leading to irresistible pressure to restore the world to the way it was before the change. The dean did his homework with the people above him, but he did not work with the members of the organization under him. He did not talk with them about the grand idea and change symbolized by the grand space. He did not make a serious effort to recruit them to try the new vision for a space with no boundaries. He did not help them anticipate and work through the change to create a sense of experimentation and excitement rather than anxiety and a distressing sense of loss.

He expected them instead to embrace it as an idea whose time had come, that is, to follow him unquestioningly and enthusiastically. This is an example of magical thinking—to approach the world as one wishes it to be rather than as it is. Unconsciously the dean experienced the faculty and staff of liberal arts as extensions of him rather than as real people with dreams and anxieties of their own. In trying to create an organization with no boundaries, he violated personal and professional boundaries, creating a space to work within that lacked any sense of the privacy that everyone needs.

As it turned out, few faculty and staff shared the dean's enthusiasm. The change felt like coercion, not consent. It felt forced rather than participatory. The change had begun with the dean's expectation that almost everyone would feel good about it, but it ended with almost everyone feeling bad about it. The university spent millions of dollars on an experiment that was doomed to failure from the outset.

It seems reasonable to speculate whether even the original design for the use of the open space was created out of ambivalence to change on the part of the dean himself. The dean wanted a vast sea of interdisciplinary relationships, but he left the traditional departments spatially intact. The faculty members of the various disciplines were placed in the space in their usual grouping, except with no walls to section off their space from that of other disciplines. Had the dean been thoroughgoing and consistent in his concept of open space, faculty would have been distributed randomly across the room. Doing so would likely have limited the exercise of traditional authority by chairs of departments, as would the lack of a place in which to exercise the authority.

Placing all the disciplines in "their area" within this big room enabled the disciplines to erect barriers, re-creating multiple departmental compounds within the open space. Instead of fulfilling the dean's fantasy of creating greater flexibility between departments and faculty, the result ultimately was just the opposite. The rigidities implicit in the separate disciplines were reinstated. Faculty and staff had the sense that in such wide open spaces, they could not feel at home. Constricting the space with furniture barriers restored the sense of home within their discipline.

Also, since it took a while to build this vast new space, everyone knew about it and how it was going to be laid out—a kind of presocialization. Resistance began to develop long before everyone moved in, giving the more agitated people on the faculty and staff time and readiness to act out. It is also worth noting that when the furniture first arrived and people started to use it to create barriers, the dean put up little or no resistance. He was unwilling to challenge this resistance to his grand vision and the implicit conflict between him and the faculty. By doing so he responded to his sense of why it might never have worked and abandoned his grand idea. Thus leadership let it happen by not acting against the resistance to change—a common reaction to resistance to change when organizations enact grand changes. Bold change agents can become gradually worn down by relentless stonewalling by employees. The unwillingness to contest and perhaps alienate the faculty resulted in reversion to the old order. The dean finally left as if in a wisp of smoke. No one missed him and many were thankful.

It is as though when faculty and staff did not immediately recognize the dean's greatness, he essentially took his ball and went home rather than stand his ground. This suggests high-order narcissism. Narcissistic leaders seek love and admiration, and as a result they are also not willing to make enemies by challenging what is going on. The dean did not act to contain the counterrevolutionary process of re-creating the old college of liberal arts. He was clueless about how to ultimately fully realize his vision. In the end the faculty and staff saw him as at once visionary, grandiose, and ineffectual. The new world order began with a bang. It ended with a whimper.

Finally, a word about different styles of change: Consultants often say you cannot communicate enough when planning and implementing change. This usually amounts to selling ideas that someone plans to impose from the top down. While this is not desirable, the leader will at least receive some feedback by taking the time to promote the change.

The implied greater transparency encourages some people to speak out, leading to the likelihood that the leader will modify the concept, thereby improving it and increasing its acceptance. This dynamic, however, usually amounts to a readily recognized process of cherry picking only those ideas that the leader thinks will improve the design. The leader ends up disregarding feedback that calls the design into question. Critical and reflective thinking that promotes questioning the design is ignored and stifled. In sum, this common approach is far short of creating change through inclusion and participation. The counterargument is that authentic inclusiveness takes longer. In fact a well-managed process of inclusion does not take longer, and it makes the implementation process more effective by reducing effort and time and avoiding exceptional levels of resistance to change. Regrettably this appreciation is lost in most organizations.

Conclusion

Before reading the stories in this section, readers might have wondered what "organizational space" has to do with the dark side of organizational experience. By now we imagine that readers will have been reminded of similar stories from their own work experience. What we have illustrated for organizational psychogeography could in fact be extended to include all organizational material culture, or artifacts.

The stories and discussion here about organizational space have explored how conscious and unconscious issues of power, authority, anxiety, abuse, loss, grandiosity, transference, and much more are played out on the stage of workplace space. The attentive organizational leader, employee, consultant, and researcher will look for this ubiquitous symbolism and ritualization, which often lie behind the veneer of mundane function and productivity. A workplace that posts "Safety First" signs everywhere may be masking heightened pressure to produce that in fact jeopardizes the safety and health of workers. In organizations, as in the rest of life, things are rarely what they seem to be at first.

PART THREE

CONCLUSIONS

We conclude our work here with two chapters. Chapter 8 provides a review of the previous chapters and stories. What have we learned while writing the book and from the stories? How do the stories as a totality provide information about the workplace, human nature, and what we suggest is the false assumption that the workplace is primarily rational in terms of how it operates? It is important to pause and examine the theory and stories for their contribution to understanding the workplace. Chapter 9 looks at how psychodynamic theory can be used to more fully understand the stories, human nature, and the workplace. In particular some theoretical perspectives offer clear insights into understanding the nature of stories and the workplace. Chapter 9 also uses theory and the stories to explore the future of the workplace. Are stories like these the norm? Is there a certain inevitability to stories such as these, that is, will they always be characteristic of the workplace? Finally, we explore how leadership might limit and avoid more stories from the dark side.

CHAPTER 8

———

The Stories, Their Meaning, and Understanding Workplace Complexity

Introduction

This one story truly stands apart from the others. It comes from a military organization. Military service also takes place in a workplace—both the battlefield and routine duty share many elements with most places of work. However, in the military the basic job is to destroy the enemy or risk being destroyed. But even in peacetime or at bases well away from the fighting, military personnel always risk having to unexpectedly engage the enemy. This story is about the confusing boundary between routine guard duty and surviving or dying.

"Ape Hangers"

This remarkable and painful-to-read story is about war, the military, honor, death, survival, and psychological trauma.

Toby was working as a motorcycle mechanic in 1970 when he briefly met Chris. Chris came to the motorcycle store to customize his new bike by adding high-rise handlebars, referred to as "ape hangers," like the ones in the 1969 film *Easy Rider*. (The handlebars get the name "ape hangers" because the rider looks like he or she is hanging from the high bars, similar to how monkeys appear when hanging on limbs or bars.) Changing the handlebars requires installing several new, much longer, cables to the front brake, throttle, and clutch—it takes some time.

Chris parked himself on some boxes of oil stacked next to where Toby would be working. He watched silently for a while before opening up a conversation. Chris and Toby immediately learned both were recently discharged Vietnam vets. Chris said that he enlisted in the army with two friends, Bill and Jim, on a buddy system. The army would keep them together thereafter. All three had made it through the worst of the fighting in the late 1960s without getting wounded or killed. They were thankful for this when they arrived at an army base, from where they were to fly home in a couple of weeks.

Chris said he and his friends were assigned to patrol the perimeter of the base. This was routine duty that, other than being hot and tiring, was boringly mundane. The days passed. One day the three of them were walking abreast when they encountered a sniper, who shot and killed Bill. One shot, one kill. After a pause Chris continued. He and Jim were back out guarding the perimeter the next day as though nothing had happened. The military puts duty first. Several more days passed before, astonishingly, Jim was also shot dead while standing next to Chris. One shot, one kill. Chris paused, then continued by saying that he was back out on patrol in the same area the next day with yet another soldier, who also was headed for home. Chris still had nearly a week left before he shipped out.

Chris told Toby this story three times before he finished the work on Chris's bike. Each time Chris added a few more details. Toby could not imagine words that would be of any comfort to Chris. The story and its repetition were extraordinarily painful to hear. As Toby listened, he figured that Chris would find it impossible to heal from this experience. Chris would no doubt carry the scars of a survivor for the rest of his life, as would Toby in some ways from hearing an unforgettable story.

Questions

In what ways can Chris's experiences be characterized as workplace trauma?

What was Toby's role in Chris's storytelling?

Why did Chris have to tell his Vietnam story three times?

In what ways are downsizing and reengineering psychologically similar to Chris's wartime trauma?

What are the psychological requirements of the listener (Toby) to stories like Chris's?

Discussion and Analysis

This is a workplace story that does not get told often enough—because few people wish to listen or tell. The story is painful for the teller and the listener. Military stories—such as from the Vietnam War, Iraq, and Afghanistan—are, after all, occupational or workplace stories. All workplaces have their risks. Patrolling the perimeter of a military base is one. Being killed by sniper fire or an improvised explosive device in Afghanistan or Iraq or a future battlefield is an occupational hazard. Suddenly losing a job as result of downsizing is another of those workplace hazards. Employees are metaphorically, if not in actuality, killed off or wounded.

Sometimes the only people who wish, and can emotionally bear, to hear such a story are those who have been through similar circumstances: active duty in World War II or Vietnam, downsizings, loss of a young child, surviving cancer, the list is endless. Toby, whose official role was to add new handlebars to Chris's motorcycle, took on several additional roles: sympathetic listener, witness, emotional container (Bion, 1962) for highly toxic material, and providing a holding environment (Winnicott, 1965) for Chris and his suffering. Some people's stories linger for years, even decades, until a person feels safe enough to share the story with someone who is likely to respond with empathy rather than defensiveness.

Then there is Chris's repetition of his story with variations. When someone has been through workplace trauma and other types of emotionally overwhelming experience, that person needs to tell and retell the story, seemingly in pursuit of some sense of mastery of what happened. Mercifully Toby knew enough not to tell Chris that he was repeating himself. Perhaps Toby also knew that words of comfort were not what Chris needed most. Chris most needed someone to be there for and with him. "Just listening" is never mere listening. It is an act of healing and an act of grace.

This story has a historical postscript. During and after the Vietnam War, the military and Veterans Administration health-care system rarely took time to help soldiers to grieve their losses or try to deal with trauma. Today the response seems to be to simply medicate the traumatized soldiers.

Finally, this story of war and death has implications for modern workplaces, where employees may not be facing bullets (at least most of the time) but nonetheless suffer trauma. Employees at all levels have stories of their suffering, and they live with the hope of finding someone who will care enough to listen to their loss and grief. This is underscored by the dark humor of one human resources professional, who said that she would be the last one out the door because she had to sign the termination forms.

Looking Back—The Stories and Their Meaning

This last story, while all too horrific in its meaning, is echoed in darkness by many stories in the earlier chapters. Sometimes death and physical injury do occur in the workplace, and as many of the stories underscored, toxic leaders, colleagues, and organizational dynamics in general can create a soul-deadening experience. Too many stories tell of employees' being rounded up by security guards and taken to a controlled location where they are terminated—and find themselves on their way home with a box of their pictures and other possessions.

What meaning may, then, be gleaned from the stories, the workplace we all experience, and human nature's sometimes uplifting, but all-too-often dark, side?

Using Stories to Explore the Dark Side of Human Nature

All of our stories illuminate the darker side of leadership, followership, and organizational life. Individually, each story provides a different view of the workplace, but taken together the stories offer pictures with consistently difficult themes. We return now to consider the five themes outlined in chapter 1.

Theme One

Our first overarching theme was that in every story, we have somewhere written or said implicitly, "You couldn't make this up," as if to reassure ourselves that these incredible experiences actually happened. We argued that taking these stories seriously means altering one's perception, definition, and experience of reality itself. In story after story leaders squander large amounts of money or fail to collect it or destroy employees' morale in order to feed their own grandiosity or sadism or to avoid looking bad to their bosses. Organizations that are ostensibly in business to make products, deliver services, and make profit often sabotage these rational goals for irrational purposes.

For instance, in one story the head of a large medical department refused to let an internal consultant and staff, who had already found ways of collecting money for one division, do the logical thing and look into the finances of other divisions to see if additional billing could also be done there. In another story, one about a large clinical laboratory, a new turnaround CEO, who was effective in marketing and selling, had quickly gained large contracts but obtained disastrous results because, in order to "save money," he would hire only temps and not full-time employees. Because the temps had not been trained to answer questions and process payments for deposit, poor service led to the loss of contracts, and many thousands of dollars' worth of payments sat in boxes full of unopened envelopes.

Theme Two

The second overarching theme in many of these organizational stories emerged from a specific kind of role the listener plays for the speaker: that of witness. In one story the consultant was a welcome presence for a midlevel manager who had come to work on a Monday, only to find the office next to her was, with no warning, terrifyingly empty. Her former colleague and his workplace possessions had simply disappeared. She finally found someone who would listen to her frightening story. In another story the new employee of a manufacturer thought he did the right thing by suggesting selling spoiled inventory to a nearby discount store to empty a warehouse so the owner would not have to build another one. However, he was terminated for having embarrassed the plant manager and consultant whom the owner had hired to run the place efficiently. Injured narcissism, rather than rationality and the quest for profit, governed the decision making.

Theme Three

The third underlying theme was part of the fabric of all the stories. The stories are embedded in a far broader and deeper context than the immediate supervisor and the specific organization. Many of the stories are embedded in the culture of the United States and express the darker side of human nature. In one story the navy continued to uncritically adhere to a regulation that led to irrational practices—such as painting a useless ship. In another story a new dean was given broad powers to design and preside over construction of a new building with an open floor plan that had disastrous results for those who occupied it. In yet a third story a Jewish CEO downsized his organization, using a methodology that resembled the selection process by Nazi officers for a temporary reprieve or immediate death in concentration camps during World War II.

Theme Four

The fourth overarching theme was the sheer power of leaders who often intimidate organization members, whose submission enables the leader to act at will. Many stories told of verbal abuse, bullying, and employees who lived in fear, if not terror. A character in one story may even have been driven to suicide. In another story a division administrator was afraid to be the first person to sit down in a new executive's office, because she had mistakenly seated herself in the previous executive's chair and was severely upbraided for doing so. In many of the stories the leader has vast power not only to get things done but also to terrorize the entire organization.

Theme Five

A final overarching theme *not* prominent in the stories is the *brighter* side of organizational life. "Pumpkin Day" is the most upbeat and heartening workplace story. Why? We think the story changes an oppressive workplace that felt like a sweatshop and prison into one in which people enjoyed coming to work, felt empowered by their leader, and were even occasionally allowed to make the workplace festive and fun, such as wearing costumes on Halloween.

Borrowing from the method used in our earlier storytelling, we now provide questions designed to provoke the reader's thoughts. Workplace themes are important to consider, spot, and reflect on.

Questions about the Stories Taken as a Whole

Which stories sounded most familiar to you?

Which stories did you find the most disturbing? Do you know why?

Which stories made most real to you the dark side of organizational life?

Which stories aroused your strongest feelings? Do you know why?

If you were a participant in any of the stories, what might you have done—or wanted to do—differently?

Can you think of any themes that we missed?

What Have We, the Authors, Learned?

As we look back on all of our stories and the chapters on method and theory, several interrelated questions come to mind: (1) What have we learned from our journey into organizational darkness? (2) What have we learned about workplaces? (3) What have we learned about our role as authors in this journey toward understanding organizations?

As we worked on the manuscript for this book, we found that our conversations had two central themes: no matter which story we told each other, it always ended with some insight into organizational darkness, and we were amazed that the events in the stories happened at all. We also observed a recurrent pattern: one story would remind us of yet another hard-to-believe story filled with organizational darkness that we had encountered during our forty-five-year careers. Some were painful to recount and others laughable, given the absurdity of the darkness and dysfunction implicit in the story. We gradually appreciated that escaping the metaphoric darkness seemed to be impossible. These dark stories, which at times had profound effects on organizations and people, had been seared into our consciousness. From our two decades of earlier collaboration and friendship, and now with these new stories, we concluded that workplaces are rarely governed exclusively by rational, objective, enlightened self-interest, productivity, efficiency, and profitability. We are confident that similar stories are carved into the memories of many of the readers of this book.

Some stories came directly from our personal experiences as employees. We began to learn from recounting our experiences at work and from writing the stories down and discussing them. Not only were they hard to believe, but they also often left a long-lasting residue of harm—a scar on the soul. They were the hot stove not to be touched twice. They were the injustices, unfairness, and personal assaults people never forget. In working with these stories, we processed and began to master them, thereby reducing their lingering traumatic effects. As we wrote these stories and explored their significance, we also validated these stories for each other. Just as our relationships with other storytellers were therapeutic, our relationship with each other was therapeutic as well as professional. Recognizing this, we understand that readers of these stories may have an opportunity to locate their own stories and hold them up for inspection and mastery as well.

Further, we gradually realized that the people who told us stories did not recount them as if they were storytelling machines but that the stories were embedded in our relationships with the people who told us their stories. Further, we realized that our role of listener was also that of *witness*—an almost sacred bestowal of a gift (Allcorn, Baum, Diamond, & Stein, 1996). In telling us their story, people felt acknowledged and validated. The relationship somehow made the story real, not just a memory.

A Brief Word on Gender in the Workplace

Many stories feature organizational leadership and interpersonal toxicity introduced by *men* in positions of power and authority. This is the case in many organizations as they still are predominantly occupied by men in leadership roles. Over the decades in which these stories were accumulated, this was truer than it is today, although women are still underrepresented in senior management roles and on boards of corporations. In this regard it is tempting to think of the problem as male. However, we want to carefully note this probably is not true when one considers that the toxicity is driven in large part by human nature, including the damage done to both male and female children by inadequate parenting that leads to deeply embedded personality disorders that produce compulsive repetition of events in early life.

Women are just as likely to introduce toxicity into the workplace as men. Namie and Namie note, "Women and men are equally likely to be bullies—exactly 50 percent each. Women bullies target women an overwhelming 84 percent of the time." (2003, p. 274). They go on to note that men target women 69 percent of the time. Therefore women are most often bullied and otherwise aggressed in the workplace. In 81 percent of all cases the bullying is by a higher-ranking individual, that is, a supervisor or higher, as illustrated in most of the stories. In sum, even though the stories address organizational toxicity and dysfunction most often created by men in powerful roles, we do not believe that it is reasonable to assume women leaders behave much differently.

We should also note that in most stories the leaders, executives, and managers are older and white, not young or members of ethnic groups. However, the stories do illustrate that some individuals who are noticeably different, such as being Jewish, can be singled out and targeted as either different or foreign, resulting in biased thoughts, feelings, and actions directed toward them.

In sum, we deeply appreciate the commonality of human nature that in many ways transcends race, sex, age, nationality, and religious diversity. Human beings are all equally likely to have experienced catastrophic caretaking as infants, children, and as young adults, sometimes creating a lifetime of personal dysfunction (Allcorn, 1992; Horney, 1950). Further, we also recognize that some deeply embedded personality dysfunctions encourage these individuals to seek out positions of power and authority and then to use that power and authority at times perversely and in self-serving ways (Babiak & Hare, 2006; Schouten & Silver, 2012).

In Conclusion

It is difficult to find an ending for the stories, a tidy way to conclude. We still have many stories left to tell. *Readers* have many stories yet to tell. And many stories are unfolding at this moment. Perhaps one way to conclude is to humbly appreciate that all these often dark stories have their origins in human nature. At any given moment the world is filled with horrific crimes against humanity and with one-on-one bullying in the workplace. If we have anything important to conclude with, it is that we hope we have underscored that the workplace is not particularly rational, and that it is filled with dark forces that have their origins in human nature—forces that most often cannot be easily managed or changed. Paradoxically, hope resides in this appreciation. Embracing the role of human nature instead of irrationally pursuing rationality at work is a first step to dealing with the dark side. We explore this sense of hope further in chapter 9, which looks to the future.

Implications for Theory and Research

The stories and this book promote inspection of the dark side of the workplace and human nature, but we also want to promote insight, acceptance, understanding, and some sense of hope. We now conclude by exploring the possibilities of understanding the workplace through storytelling as well as the inherent psychodynamic nature of storytelling. Hope lies in the healing ability of storytelling and the learning potential it creates, but realizing these benefits requires a grasp of the theoretical nature and complexity of storytelling. In the first chapter we alluded to many aspects of storytelling and located it within a larger context of theoretical and academic knowledge. We now turn to a more in-depth exploration of the theory behind the stories—the rest of the story. We begin by discussing theory that we then ground in a short story to illustrate how the theory applies to stories. We conclude by adding a few further reflections on the contribution that stories make to the workplace.

Using Psychodynamic Theory to Understand Storytelling

The nature of the relationship between the storyteller and the story listener is one of asymmetric co-creation: what is created contains unconscious and conscious elements that intertwine, much like a DNA molecule, to define storyteller and listener and the meaning of the story. The story emerges from memory and contains conscious and unconscious qualities that are filtered through thought to become spoken. The words and story are in a sense placed upon a surface (like writing on a white board) before the story listener. The listener brings to the story conscious and unconscious propensities as to how the words and their combinations are heard. This transforms the words into a story in a unique way with its origins deep within the listener. Storytelling and listening may then be understood to take place within potential space filled with creative telling and listening. The storyteller and story listener become the co-creators of the story. The story may be conceived of as an object in a place between the storyteller and the listener that, while asymmetrically constructed by the storyteller, is also influenced by the listener, who helps to create the potential space by being there to listen. The listener also influences the telling by using various forms of communication such as body language, laughter, or verbal questions and encouragement. To fulfill this role the story listener should stifle any impulses to interrupt or cut off the story-teller. Thus the story listener must be a good enough listener to make it safe, fun, and playful for the storyteller to put the story into the space between them.

The nature of this dynamic is grounded in psychoanalytic theory. We briefly explore two notions—Thomas Ogden's description of the "intersubjective analytic third" and Donald Winnicott's innovation of the "squiggle game," which makes a child feel safe enough to communicate with a therapist.

Ogden's Analytic Third

Ogden's conception of the analytic third offers insight into the underlying nature of the stories. His notion is complementary to our discussion of storytelling and listening, as in creating a world around a campfire at night. The teller and the listener join together in the interpersonal field between them. Ogden writes, "In an analytic relationship, the notion of individual subjectivity and the idea of a co-created third subject are devoid of meaning except in relation to one another, just as the idea of the conscious mind is meaningless except in relation to the unconscious" (Ogden, 1999).

This perspective is consistent with our approach to understanding the nature of storytelling and listening, in that the story as it is told is located in interpersonal space where the story is co-created consciously and unconsciously between the teller and listener. To this may be added, "While both analyst and analysand participate in the creation and elaboration of the unconscious analytic third, they do so asymmetrically" (Ogden, 1999). The storyteller situates the story "out there" for the listener(s), consuming in the moment most of the airtime while also providing most of the content. In this regard the co-creation in the interpersonal space is asymmetrical.

We also suggest that the co-creation of the story in this interpersonal space is a dynamic process, with the story ever changing, as it is told and recalled and understood. Ogden writes, "I view the intersubjective analytic third as an ever-changing unconscious third subject (more verb than noun) which powerfully contributes to the structure of the analytic relationship. The analyst's and patient's experience in and of the analytic third spans the full range of human emotion and its attendant thoughts, fantasies, bodily sensations, and so on" (Ogden, 1999). The story as told and asymmetrically co-created in interpersonal space gradually takes on a life of its own. Every listener and teller creates the monster beyond the light of the campfire as an act of fantastic creation unencumbered in the moment by reality. This co-creation becomes part of the seamless, inter-woven fabric of the story. The meaning of the story becomes unique to each listener, but at the same time it is a part of the co-creation process within interpersonal space.

How, then, may the would-be organizational theorist, scholar, or re-searcher understand the telling and listening? Ogden writes, "The task of the analyst is to create conditions in which the unconscious intersubjec-tive analytic third (which is always multi-layered and multi-faceted and continually on the move) might be experienced, attached to words, and eventually spoken about with the analysand" (Ogden, 1999). This is a challenging task to take up not only in therapy but also in understanding the story as it exists between the teller and listener. This is compounded by the presence of other listeners.

Many questions arise. Why was it important for the teller to tell the story? How does it relate to the teller's life, thoughts, and feelings in the moment? How did the teller come to locate the story in the moment given the presence of the listener? What challenges did the listener expe-rience, such as wanting to interrupt the teller by telling a different story? How did the listener influence the telling by listening? And what story did the listener actually hear, and how did it differ from the story the teller told? These are only some of the challenges to understanding the conscious and unconscious elements of storytelling.

What Ogden says of the analyst applies equally to the organizational scholar, researcher or consultant in understanding organizations and storytelling. Ogden suggests,

> For the analyst, this means relying to a very large degree on "the foul rag-and-bone shop" (Yeats, 1936/1966, p. 336) of his reverie experience (his mundane, everyday thoughts, feelings, ruminations, preoccupations, daydreams, bodily sensations, and so forth). The analyst's use of his reverie experience requires tolerance of the experience of not knowing, of finding himself (or, perhaps more accurately, losing himself) adrift and apparently directionless. (Ogden, 1999)

These considerations suggest that the listener, observer, or participant must be able to attend to one's own internal thoughts and feelings, in addition to attending to what is happening between the two people, for in them lie insights into the teller, the listener, and the story.

A final consideration is the nature of the analytic third with its unconscious origins and perhaps only partially conscious and discussable content. Ogden identifies three scenarios with the analytic third in psychotherapy. Of the first two scenarios he writes,

> Often, in my experience, the "third subject" is of a subjugating sort which creates the effect of tyrannically limiting the range of thoughts, feelings, and bodily sensations 'permissible' to both analyst and analysand. Under such circumstances, neither analyst nor analysand is able to experience himself or the other in terms outside of a very narrow band of (predominantly irrational) thoughts and feelings. At other times, the analytic third is of a perverse sort that has the effect of locking the analyst and patient into a specific, compulsively repeated perverse scenario. (Ogden, 1999)

He continues, describing the third scenario:

At still other times, the analytic third may be of a powerfully creative and enriching sort. Such forms of the analytic third are enlivening in the sense that "shapes" are generated in the analytic relationship (for instance, interesting, sometimes novel, forms of considering, dreaming, and fantasizing as well as richer and more fully human qualities of object relatedness marked, for example, by humor, compassion, playfulness, flirtatiousness, camaraderie, charm, love, and anger which have "all the sense of real" [Winnicott, 1965, p. 184]. (Ogden, 1999)

Ogden's three scenarios within the analytic third (in therapy) offer insights into storytelling and listening. The storyteller and the listener can come to share consciously and unconsciously a sense of tyranny, mystery, myth, horror, and threat. The co-creation can end up creating a straight-jacket of interpersonal terror. Conversely the outcome may be one of playful and joyful sharing, understanding, mutual respect and coevolution of the story as well as its meaning. Ogden writes,

Rather, as is the case with transferences, in the course of the analysis of a given form of pathological analytic third, the capacity of the third to timelessly hold the analytic pair hostage in a given, unchanging, unconscious form of relatedness (or unrelatedness) is gradually transmuted into forms of experience of self and other that can be preconsciously and consciously experienced, verbally symbolized, reflected upon, spoken about and incorporated into one's larger sense of self (including one's experience of and understanding of how one has come to be who one is and who one is becoming). (Ogden, 1999)

Is this not ultimately what the telling, sharing, listening, and understanding of stories are ultimately about? These three perspectives are discussed further in the next section as three scenarios for storytelling and listening.

Three Scenarios of Storytelling and Story Listening
The three figures that follow occupy the space between us as authors and you as readers. By providing them we hope to communicate a visual-

ization of how the theory may be applied in practice. Each figure locates an I and a you.

In figure 1 the creative, playful analytic third (Ogden's third scenario) might be imagined as a piece of paper or whiteboard (for black markers), the meeting point of I and you, two intersubjective "force fields" akin to gravity or electromagnetism. In the creative third space, the people in the space are dominant, and the relationship liberates creativity and possibility. The sense of the space is one of safe enough holding and potential space (Winnicott, 1965).

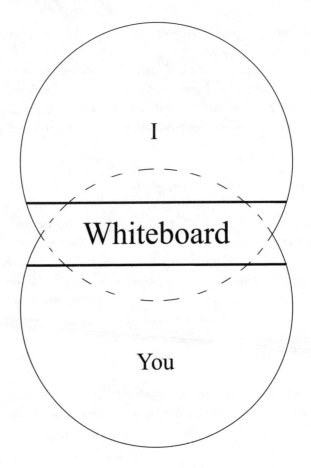

Figure 1. Creative Third

In contrast Ogden's subjugating, tyrannical third (his first scenario) is experienced as persecutory space. Imagine the two people in the subjugating third as imprisoned behind heavy bars (see figure 2). In this analytic third, space is dominant and feels oppressive, constraining, confining, and even suffocating, as if one is in a cell. The prison is filled with taboos and secrets and bad faith, with many things that cannot be said—or even thought. Stories feel as though they have been imposed in this space. Perhaps Jean-Paul Sartre's play *No Exit* (1955) embodies this tyrannical third. If in the creative third the story listener uses the potential space between storyteller and listener to empower the previously unempowered storyteller to tell the story, in the subjugating third the story listener seizes and takes away the storyteller's authority and power, and in doing so severely narrows the story that can be told. To the storyteller the story listener feels judgmental, not available, or absent. The storyteller also contributes to this dynamic by becoming defensive, withdrawn, or resigned and less willing to tell the story as well as less accessible to the listener. Together they create a largely undiscussable context in which

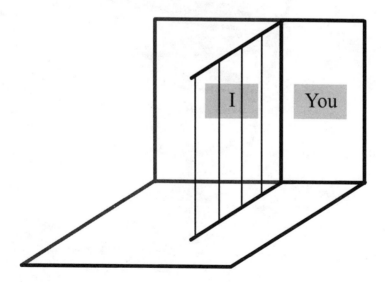

Figure 2. Tyrannical Third

they maintain a sense of being subjugated to the quality of the space they have created. There is, as symbolized by the bars, no apparent or easy-to-access escape in the moment.

Finally, there is the perverse third (Ogden's second scenario), characterized by endless repetition. All stories are essentially the same and must be repeated, that is, they have an involuntary, compulsively repetitive, and controlling character. The image that comes to mind is a spiral. If creative space nurtures the creation of virtuous cycles of listening, telling, and co-creation, perverse space imposes a vicious cycle, a vicious and endless spiral that ends with itself and from which there seems to be no escape (see figure 3). The perverse third is a world of changelessness. One thinks of the aphorism that insanity is defined as doing the same thing over and over while expecting different results.

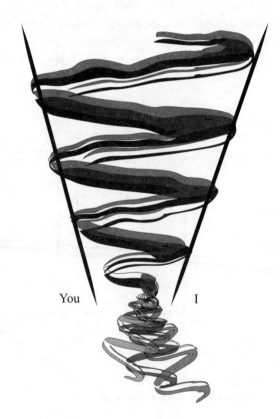

Figure 3. Perverse Third

We conclude our discussion of this theory with an illustrative story that, as it unfolds, illustrates all three forms the analytic third can take.

Jessica had already worked two decades as a midlevel manager at ABC Corporation. She was widely recognized as a reliable, hard worker. She consistently outperformed many of her peers. She had won several outstanding manager awards over the years. She was a quiet, effective leader of her employees. Still, she also was consistently passed over for pay raises and promotions. She had experienced some occasional bullying, ridicule, intimidation, and emotional abuse, from many of her male and female superiors.

In recent years she had tried talking with various supervisors and executives about her experiences but to no avail. She had looked for other jobs from time to time but was rejected as overqualified and gradually, it seemed, too old to hire. Recently out of desperation she made an appointment with the corporate CEO, Mary, who professed to have an open-door policy. Jessica felt Mary was her last hope.

Jessica approached her interview with high hopes that Mary would be a receptive, sympathetic listener. In her imagination Jessica thought that since both she and Mary were women, Mary would be particularly understanding of Jessica's experience. Maybe Mary would even help remedy Jessica's situation.

Mary greeted Jessica and welcomed her into the office. They sat in comfortable armchairs facing each other. Mary began by saying, "Jessica, I understand you want to discuss some issues with me. Tell me what's on your mind." Encouraged, Jessica told her story. At first Mary was attentive, facing her, mostly looking directly at Jessica's face. Mary encouraged Jessica to take her time—saying she had set aside half an hour for the visit. She asked Jessica only a few questions but mostly listened, nodding her head.

After perhaps ten minutes, Mary's attention seemed to diminish. She seemed to be getting nervous or becoming unsettled. She looked as if her mind was wandering off the conversation. Mary occasionally shifted position in her chair while trying to look keenly interested in what Jessica had to say.

Jessica noticed this and spoke faster, more urgently, pressing her case. Jessica began to wonder whether Mary was still interested in her story.

Occasionally now Mary would look around her office and glance at her wristwatch. About fifteen minutes into the visit the executive vice president for finance opened the door to Mary's office and hurriedly walked toward Mary. Mary abruptly cut Jessica off, saying, "The vice president needs to meet with me in the conference room." She then said, looking back over her shoulder to Jessica as she left, "We women have to stick together!"

Jessica found herself alone and then walked down the hall to her office. Jessica felt ejected, rejected, confused. She didn't know what to make of the visit, which had seemed to start so cordially. She never again heard from Mary. Nothing changed, and she felt it had been a mistake to even consider telling Mary her story.

Discussion and Analysis of Story

Let us try to make sense of Jessica's story with the help of the three storyteller–story listener scenarios and their corresponding types of analytic thirds, which we identified earlier. The visit seems to have begun with good emotional attunement between Mary and Jessica. Jessica felt emotionally held and contained in a respectful, compassionate relationship. Her conversation with Mary brimmed with hope and possibility. After about ten minutes Mary's attention and interest seemed to wane. She became unreceptive and unavailable. Jessica felt herself becoming more desperate and tried even harder to make her case. She felt increasingly trapped in a tyrannical, emotionally frozen space. What had begun as an open, creative space now felt constricted, imprisoning, confining. Jessica was now a prisoner in her own story.

Soon Jessica began to feel a sense of déjà vu. She had been in similar circumstances before, where her colleagues and superiors claimed to want to hear her but soon made clear they were not interested. In short, Jessica was in yet another loop of the vicious downward spiral of repetition. Her sense of Mary was further confirmed when the executive vice president entered the office—was this not protected time for Jessica?—and Mary summarily ended the conversation. Mary left Jessica with the empty platitude "we women have to stick together." The remark did not feel reassuring to Jessica. She felt ejected from the office and rejected, thrust out into the hallway. Her hope had turned into distress, leading to a dismissive platitude.

In sum, in a single episode of storytelling and story listening, Jessica experienced all three scenarios of creative, imprisoning, and repetitive thirds. We suggest that the model offers a framework for understanding the psychic reality, or unconscious experience, of storytelling and story listening as stories are often the means of communication in the workplace.

We now examine Winnicott's squiggle approach to therapy with children for its contribution to understanding the psychodynamic nature of storytelling.

Winnicott and Squiggles, Holding Environments, and Potential Space

Winnicott developed the squiggle game and used it in pediatric psychotherapy. Jean Thurow (1989) writes,

> Winnicott's premise is that personality growth and change have their roots in the early matrix of the child and the maternal care. Therapy, for Winnicott, is a process that re-establishes the interactive process, begun in earliest infancy, at that point where it had become disrupted. Just as the self was formed as a result of interaction between the infant and the mother (who represents the environment), so the ongoing development of the self can be re-established as a result of interactions between the self and the therapist (who also represents the environment). This is the crux of therapeutic change. The squiggle game, with its interactional structure, its physical "holding" environment, and its offering of a useable object for use in communication, becomes a graphic illustration of Winnicott's therapeutic model. (Thurow, 1989)

The squiggle game, wherein the child and therapist take turns adding to a drawing, informs our understanding of storytelling and story listening as both are involved with communication, symbolizing, and revealing oneself within a safe-enough context. This context is the space between—for example, the piece of paper on which the squiggle is created or a flip chart or whiteboard in a corporate meeting—interpersonal space that is experienced as safe and even playful but is also a product of co-creation. Like the squiggle game, stories, storytelling, and story listening are potentially, if not actually, therapeutic. In the setting of telling and listening, not unlike Winnicott's squiggles, there exists a sense of personal openness, trust of the listener, a sense of being listened to and valued. Further, in both storytelling and psychotherapy, the squiggle game creates and sustains the analytic third.

The squiggle may be further understood to implicitly or explicitly create a holding environment and potential space where play and creativity arise (Winnicott, 1965). A safe-enough holding environment is, for example, the soothing and comforting experience created by a mother holding her infant. This can also be achieved in the workplace, usually by a leader but also by a group that creates a safe-enough interpersonal space that reduces anxiety and allows everyone to focus on problem solving and creating new ideas. In this potential space, people can exchange ideas without fear and vulnerability. Storytelling may also help to create the safe-enough holding context, promote learning, and foster a playful exploration of possibilities.

Stories as Information, Training, and Leadership

As we discussed in chapter 2, stories also nicely serve applied and utilitarian purposes. Telling a story in response to encountering a significant operating problem or other challenge can create not only a holding environment and potential space but the playful creative third. After listening to individuals or groups lay out a major workplace problem, one of us found that he could consistently locate a similar situation in his experience and tell a story that included how the problem arose, how it was tackled, and the outcome. The story contained attention to reflectivity, careful data collection and analysis, a search for solutions, and one or more of the challenges of implementing the response, along with monitoring the outcome to ensure it resolved the problem. What was interesting about telling these stories was that it led the individual or group to follow the process, feeling that it was safe enough to explore the problem and solution in potential space. Even more interesting was the fact that the story told was often remembered *by the listeners* even in its details years later, providing a safe-enough mental context to use the processes that resided within the story to solve other operating problems. This outcome seemed to be much more effective than a lecture on problem solving.

We now turn our attention to exploring whether the dark side of organizational life may be moderated, mediated, and its unconscious underpinning even minimized, at least for a period of time. In order to do this we feel obliged to once again acknowledge the powerful effects human nature has on the workplace and how one experiences it. There is no getting around this fact. We do, however, believe the brighter side of human nature can be encouraged to express itself.

Beyond Organizational Darkness: Good-Enough Leadership

In most of the stories we have portrayed the implacable darkness, even bleakness, in much of contemporary organizational life, driven by unconscious elements resident in human nature. We have suggested that the workplace is not often managed in an ideal fashion, where rationality and objectivity produce profit, and individuals invariably logically pursue their own economic self-interest. Although the gaps in this idealized image of leaders and of individual and organizational performance produce darkness, they also open the door to creativity, new connections and insights, and the possibility of change if they are not quashed by management. This potential is always latent and can be realized. In a world characterized by a hard leadership style that is top-down, controlling, and often emotionally brutal, this creative potential is often stifled. New ideas are not only unwelcome; they can be career-ending ideas if expressed. In the final section we offer the possibility and hope that organizational life is not condemned to darkness, when leaders help to contain the darker elements while creating a safe-enough playful space for work and creativity. If there is hope that is not grounded in baseless or irrational optimism, what would it look like? How would it work in reality?

That hope rests on a concept we are calling good-enough leadership (Stein & Allcorn, 2014). The good-enough leader is open, considerate, a good listener, and provides clear direction while also being inclusive in decision making and implementation. To the good-enough leader, people are sentient, separate beings to be respected, not things to be manipulated and disposed of. People are valued for what they do and who they are.

The good-enough leader is capable of making and implementing difficult decisions, but only after she or he has gathered thoughts, feelings, ideas, and concerns from colleagues and subordinates. Good-enough leadership is characterized by the core values of openness, inclusiveness, transparency, collaboration, trust, and respect. In this atmosphere people accomplish organizational tasks enthusiastically because of the openness and inclusivity—compared to the more commonly encountered secretiveness and unilateralism—of the leader.

The good-enough leadership style rests in turn on two central psychological processes and qualities in the leader, those of containment (Bion, 1961) and of serving as a holding environment (Winnicott, 1965). The literature on these concepts is extensive, and we discussed some of it in chapter 2. For our purposes here, think of a container as a vessel that does not break, explode, or expel whatever is poured into it but rather serves as a receptacle that keeps the contents for a while. Of course the human container is not made of glass or baked clay but of empathy and the capacity for reflection. The human container is curious about what he or she has taken in from the other person or group and is not broken or destroyed by it.

Here is where the idea of a holding environment comes in: the kind of human container one is. During a baby's infancy the mother or other caretaker both physically and emotionally holds on to the baby. The caretaker receives the baby's anxieties and terrors and responds in a good-enough way that the baby feels held, understood, cared for, and nourished. In the process the baby feels soothed and reassured, so the baby can go on living without fear of annihilation, falling apart, or abandonment.

The good-enough leader does not literally contain or hold the organization but rather performs these emotional functions symbolically—through words, documents, e-mails, body language, tone of voice, facial expression, metaphors, storytelling, arrangement of office furniture, availability, and so on. Ultimately in the experience of organizational life these are far more emotionally valent and enduring than mission and vision statements, strategic plans, and Excel spreadsheets. The emotional life of organizations (Diamond, 1993) is an inseparable part of the day-to-day activities, productivity, profitability, and reality of an organization. The leadership style is a large part of "what it is like to work here."

Let us offer two concluding stories that will starkly contrast the more common top-down, command and control, unilateral style of leadership and good-enough leadership.

STORY 1

A powerful hospital CEO assembled in an auditorium about seventy-five senior executives and midlevel managers. He began by telling a story about the declining fortunes and revenue of the hospital and said some hard choices were ahead—most imminent of all, downsizing. He said: "Imagine that you are on a train station platform. There are two trains approaching. I will get on the first train, which takes you to the destination I have planned. You can either get on that train with me or wait for the next train and take your chances where it will go. You decide."

The auditorium was filled with anxious silence. Most people in the room resolved their anxiety by using the common defense mechanism of identifying with the aggressor. As a result the CEO had their submission and obedience. He could proceed with impunity with his dramatic plans for hospital downsizing that ultimately would sweep up some of those consenting. He did not contain their anxiety. Rather he used fear and intimidation to achieve submission. He did not serve as a holding environment but relied on—exploited—his audience's heightened anxiety to direct it toward his goals. He counted on their induced regression to make them malleable. He was all-powerful, and in his mind and in their own minds they changed from real people into potential "organizational fat" that had to be removed.

STORY 2

A hospital CEO assembled about seventy-five senior and midlevel managers for a meeting in an auditorium. He said dramatically that the hospital had lost revenue recently and that costs would have to be cut. He showed an impressive array of PowerPoint spreadsheets that documented unmistakably how dire the hospital's financial situation was. He said the only solution was to immediately reduce costs by eliminating hospital personnel. Those present would simply have to determine who would be laid off and implement the downsizing.

When he finished his presentation, silent anxiety pervaded the room. He then asked if anyone had questions. Several people asked operational and procedural questions, such as specifically how to implement the plan, how many people would have to be laid off, the time line, and so on. After a while one executive raised her hand and was recognized by the CEO. She said: "Your solution is to *cut costs*. I wonder whether there might be ways to *increase revenue* instead." Suddenly the sullen, depressed group came alive with ideas about how to increase revenue. They felt hope and empowered by the executive's audacious idea. Several weeks later the CEO issued a memorandum saying that he was forming a committee to look into ways to increase hospital revenue.

What had happened to so dramatically change the emotional climate in the room? The executive who raised the question about revenue had first taken in—contained—the dismal economic news and felt the palpable dread in the room. She then functioned briefly as a holding environment to emotionally hold on to and process what had been taking place (rather than simply and defensively react). She then offered an interpretation or recommendation that helped the other employees to feel empowered and in turn to diminish their anxiety. Although she was not the CEO, she temporarily served in the group as a good-enough leader. Subsequently the CEO's memorandum affirmed that pursuing new revenue sources rather than automatically resorting to mass firings had been a worthwhile idea.

These two stories illustrate the difference between traditional top-down leadership and good-enough leadership. If there is a way out of pervasive organizational darkness, it will be through emotionally available, reflective leaders who can contain, hold on to, and process the anxiety that arises in any organization. The stories we have told in this book do not have to be the inevitable future of organizational life. There is hope that good-enough leaders can make a difference.

How Can You Step into the Role of Good-Enough Leader?

We want to provide a few reflections on how someone may take up good-enough leadership. Much depends on one's willingness to be reflective and self-aware. In saying this we assume a good-enough leadership role is one of the more challenging things to undertake. However, we also suggest that it can be one of the more rewarding ones as well. We offer the following thoughts, which we hope will encourage and contribute to readers' taking up the good-enough leadership role.

- Take the time to do a little reading on leadership in general, to better understand how good-enough leadership differs from much of what is written about leadership. This is important because others who use traditional top-down methods will observe that you are not leading their way and will challenge and criticize your leadership. In fact some may not have a clue how good-enough leadership works.

• Be prepared to be seen as an outlier and contrarian by your peers and superiors in terms of your different leadership style. This reaction is likely to stand in contrast to the positive experience of those you are leading. They are likely to share their positive experience with others throughout the organization. In fact people from other divisions may seek to move into your area.

• Not all those whom you lead may like the good-enough style, preferring to be told what to do and subjected to close monitoring. In many instances coaching can overcome these feelings but not always, and good-enough leaders are supportive of employees who prefer traditional leadership styles and wish to change jobs.

• Your work as a good-enough leader also takes the form of passing it along—training subordinates to take up the style themselves, improving their management, supervisory, and leadership styles. In this regard "walking the talk" is much more important in terms of passing it along than telling people what to do. A good role model is one of the best of all educational and learning opportunities.

• When you move on, you should be prepared for the individual who replaces you to return your area of responsibility to a top-down and unilateral style, including allowing the dark forces to reemerge in the process. Your former employees may communicate to you a very real sense of loss, as the safe-enough third space and its creative and playful qualities are stripped away, sometimes with a vengeance. We can only alert you to this and encourage acceptance. It has happened to us.

Conclusion

We hope that this book and its stories have made the point that the workplace is not-so-rational, reasonable, or fair, and that the dark side of human nature is always present, creating performance-robbing organizational dysfunction and human casualties. We have also provided a few stories in which someone overcame these dark forces and dysfunctions, and leaders created not only an exciting and productive workplace but also an emotionally safe-enough place to work, where reflectivity and creativity were not only possible but rewarded. These outcomes were achieved by good-enough leadership. Having said this, most of the stories and our experience in the workplace as executives, employees, consultants, and researchers seem to impress upon us how omnipresent, powerful, persistent, and damaging the dark forces can be at work.

Will the Dark Forces Invariably Predominate?

This is a challenging question. Our answer is a qualified yes. In applying psychodynamic theory, reading clinical and workplace case studies, general observation in the workplace, including firsthand experience, and of course a vast array of news (ranging from fraud that destroys life savings for retirement to global events, as evidenced by the collapse of the financial industry in 2007 and 2008 after a feeding frenzy on securitized mortgage instruments), we find that the dark forces are omnipresent and highly energized. Social destruction driven by rampant self-interest and greed, lack of or absence of regulation, and an easily preyed-upon population create a context that nurtures the dark forces and all too often allows them to bloom. Predation takes so many forms that the possibilities are nearly endless, ranging from taking advantage of the aged by selling them defective products and services all the way up to executives of large corporations duped into taking actions that create financially catastrophic results. To these considerations we add another important one.

The high drive of these predators in the workplace may also limit and even wipe out other leaders who try their best to be good-enough leaders—effective, thoughtful, reflective managers. By acting in this way these good-enough leaders predispose themselves to predation and elimination, which is especially likely if the predators are either in higher organizational roles or are supported and defended by individuals in senior roles. In our experience and research the most aggressive, self-seeking individuals often present themselves in a way that is admired because they take charge and "kick ass," especially in organizations with boards that think the company needs to be shaken up. It is not hard to find examples of organizations whose boards have empowered the CEO to make sweeping changes by almost any means necessary, including removing most of those in senior management roles, effecting sweeping reorganizations, and downsizing. While the CEO appears not to be making the decisions about who is to be laid off, the people terminated are often not regarded as team players this CEO can dominate. In particular anyone who appears to question the CEO's grandiosity and omnipotence must go.

With a degree of sadness we are of the view that the dark forces often win out over more enlightened forms of leadership, including good-enough leaders. However, we wish to add that this is not always true, and effective leaders, like good-enough leaders, can be found leading large organizations and creating new ones, as well as leading subdivisions of large organizations where their leadership creates a counterculture—one that regrettably is viewed with suspicion by leaders of other divisions and senior management. Often this deviating difference is seen as a threat that has to be contained or eliminated (Allcorn, 1991). We note the maxim often attributed to Edmund Burke, although the author remains unknown: "The only thing necessary for the triumph of evil is for good men to do nothing."

In writing this book we suggest that an in-depth appreciation of the dark side of organizations better prepares those in leadership roles to be good-enough leaders. It gives them the insight to better appreciate the dark side and in turn to be better able to defend against its toxic effects. Understanding that it is there in the first place replaces fantasies and myths that organizations are operated on a rational basis and reward good performance. In a sense, being armed with this knowledge is a major first step in fending off the predators and toxic and destructive behavior that may be focused on those who are perceived to be vulnerable and soft targets—other managers and executives who practice good-enough leadership. Having said this, it remains our view that the inherent vulnerability that resides in being thoughtful, reflective, fair, and reasonable is most often no match for the high energy levels and exceptional persistence that characterize the dark forces. This is the challenge that faces those who strive to be effective, humane leaders. The challenge will always be great but not insurmountable.

References

Adams, G., & Balfour, D. (2009). *Unmasking administrative evil* (3rd ed.). Armonk, NY: Sharpe.

Allcorn, S. (1991). *Workplace superstars in resistant organizations.* Westport, CT: Quorum Books.

Allcorn, S. (1992). *Codependency in the workplace.* Westport, CT: Quorum Books.

Allcorn, S. (2002). *Death of the spirit in the American workplace.* Westport, CT: Quorum Books.

Allcorn, S., Baum, H., Diamond, M., & Stein, H. (1996). *The human cost of a management failure: Downsizing at General Hospital.* Westport, CT: Quorum Books.

Argyris, C. (1982). *Reasoning, learning and action.* San Francisco: Jossey-Bass.

Armstrong, D. (1992). *Managing by storying around.* New York: Doubleday.

Babiak, P., & Hare, R. (2006). *Snakes in suits: When psychopaths go to work.* New York: Harper.

Bion, W. (1961). *Experience in groups.* London: Tavistock.

Bion, W. (1962). A theory of thinking. *International Journal of Psycho-Analysis, 43,* 306–310.

Bollas, C. (1989). *The Shadow of the object: Psychoanalysis of the unthought known.* New York: Columbia.

Czander, W. (1993). *The psychodynamics of work and organizations.* New York: Guilford.

Devereux, G. (1956). Normal and abnormal: The key problem of psychiatric anthropology. In J. Casagrande & T. Gladwin (Eds.), *Some uses of anthropology: Theoretical and applied.* (pp. 23–48). Washington, DC: Anthropological Society of Washington.

215

Diamond, M. (1986). Resistance to change: A psychoanalytic critique of Argris and Schon's contributions to organizational theory and intervention. *Journal of Management Studies, 23*(5), 543–562.

Diamond, M. (1993). *The unconscious life of organizations.* Westport, CT: Quorum.

Erikson, E. (1968). *Identity: Youth and crisis.* New York: Norton.

Fornari, F. (1975). *The psychoanalysis of war* (A. Pfeifer, Trans.). Bloomington: University of Indiana Press. (Original work published 1966)

Fromm, E. (1970). Thoughts on bureaucracy. *Management Science, 16*(12), 699–705.

Gabriel, Y. (1999). *Organizations in depth.* London: Sage.

Gabriel, Y. (2011, October 12). Stories and storytelling in organizations and research [Web log post]. Retrieved from http://www.yiannisgabriel.com/2011/10/stories-and-storytelling-in.html

Gabriel, Y. (2012). Organizations in a state of darkness: Towards a theory of organizational miasma. *Organization Studies, 33*(9), 1137–1152.

Goodman, N., & Meyers, M. (2012). *The power of witnessing: Reflections, reverberations, and traces of the Holocaust: Trauma, psychoanalysis, and the living mind.* New York: Routledge.

Hilberg, R. (1993). *Perpetrators victims bystanders: The Jewish catastrophe, 1933–1945.* New York: Harper.

Horney, K. (1950). *Neurosis and human growth: The struggle toward self-realization.* New York: Norton.

Hummel, R. (1991). Stories managers tell: Why they are as valid as science. *Public Administration Review, 51*(1), 31–41.

James, C., & Minnis, W. (2004). Organizational storytelling: It makes sense. *Business Horizons, 47*(4), 23–32.

Kellerman, B. (2004). *Bad leadership: What it is, how it happens, why it matters.* Boston: Harvard Business School.

Kets de Vries, M. (2006). *The leader on the couch: A clinical approach to changing people and organizations.* San Francisco: Jossey-Bass.

Kohut, H. (1971). *The analysis of the self.* New York: International Universities Press.

Levinson, H. (1962). *Men, management, and mental health.* Cambridge, MA: Harvard University Press.

Mitscherlich, A., & Mitscherlich, M. (1975). *The inability to mourn: Principles of collective behavior*. New York: Grove Press.

Namie, G., & Namie, R. (2003). *The bully at work*. Naperville, IL: Sourcebooks.

Ogden, T. (1999). The analytic third: An overview. Retrieved from http://www.psychspace.com/psych/viewnews-795

Peters, T., & Waterman, R. (1982). *In search of excellence*. New York: Random House.

Pollock, T., & Bono, J. (2013). Being Scheherazade: The importance of storytelling in academic writing. *Academy of Management Journal, 56*(3), 629–634.

Schein, E. (2010). *Organizational culture and leadership*. (4th ed.). San Francisco: Jossey-Bass.

Schouten, R., & Silver, J. (2012). *Almost a psychopath: Do I (or does someone I know) have a problem with manipulation and lack of empathy?* Boston: Harvard University.

Shengold. L. (1991). *Soul murder: The effects of childhood abuse and deprivation*. New York: Ballantine.

Silver-Greenberg, J., Protess, B., & Barboza, D. (2013, August 17). Hiring in China by JPMorgan under scrutiny. *New York Times*. Retrieved from http://dealbook.nytimes.com/2013/08/17/hiring-in-china-by-jpmorgan-under-scrutiny/?hp

Smith, P. (2012). *Lead with a story: A guide to crafting business narratives that captivate, convince, and inspire*. New York: AMACOM.

Spence, D. (1982). *Narrative truth and historical truth: Meaning and interpretation in psychoanalysis*. New York: Norton.

Stein, H. (1994). *Listening deeply*. Boulder, CO: Westview Press.

Stein, H. (2001). *Nothing personal, just business*. Westport, CT: Quorum Books.

Stein, H. (2013). *Developmental Time, Cultural Space: Studies in psychogeography* (2nd ed.). New York: Library of Social Science.

Stein, H., & Allcorn, S. (2014). Good enough leadership: A model of leadership. *Organisational and Social Dynamics, 14*(2), 342–366.

Stein, H., & Apprey, M. (1990). *Clinical stories and their translations*. Charlottesville: University Press of Virginia.

Stein, H., & Niederland, W. (Eds.). (1989). *Maps from the mind: Readings in psychogeography*. Norman: University of Oklahoma Press.

Thurow, J. (1989). Interactional squiggle drawings with children: An illustration of the therapeutic change process. *Focusing Folio, 8*(4), 149–186. Retrieved from https://www.focusing.org/chfc/articles/en/thurow-interaction-squiggle-total.htm

Volkan, V. (1988). *The need to have enemies and allies: From clinical practice to international relationships.* Northvale, NJ: Jason Aronson.

Volkan, V. (1997). *Blood lines: From ethnic pride to ethnic terrorism.* New York: Farrar, Straus and Giroux.

Volkan, V. (2001). Transgenerational transmissions and chosen traumas: An aspect of large-group identity. *Group Analysis, 34*(1), 79–97.

Volkan, V. (2004). *Blind trust: Large groups and their leaders in times of crisis and terror.* Charlottesville, VA: Pitchstone.

Volkan, V. (2005, December). Large-group identity and chosen trauma. *Psychoanalysis Downunder: The Online Journal of the Australian Psychoanalytic Society, 6.* Retrieved from http://www.psychoanalysis-downunder.com.au/downunder/issues/6/papers/81

Volkan, V. (2006). *Killing in the name of identity: A study of bloody conflicts.* Charlottesville, VA: Pitchstone.

White, M., & Epton, D. (1990). *Narrative means to therapeutic ends.* New York: Norton.

Winnicott, D. (1965). *The maturational processes and the facilitating environment: Studies in the theory of emotional development.* London: Hogarth Press.

Index